Prop

Prophets and Saints

T. L. VASWANI

Crest Publishing House
(A JAICO ENTERPRISE)
G - 2, 16 Ansari Road, Darya Ganj
New Delhi - 110002.

PROPHETS AND SAINTS
ISBN 81-242-0063-7

First Paperback Impression : 2002

Published by:
CREST PUBLISHING HOUSE
(A Jaico Enterprise)
G-2, 16 Ansari Road
Darya Ganj, New Delhi-110002

Printed by:
Gayatri Offset Press
A-66, Sector-2, Noida-201301

Foreword

The Essays brought together in this book were written at different times.

The subjects in which an increasing number of India's youths seem to take growing interest are birth-control and politics. Their deeper values, I submit, may be considered in the light of Religion and Social Reconstruction. So I invite India's youths to study the lives of the world's prophets and saints: only a few of them are presented in this volume. Many more may be studied in the "East and West Series."

Rishi Dayanand has long remained, almost, a lonely figure: his loneliness is a tribute to his "greatness." This "prophet of reform," like some other truly great ones in India and other countries, pleaded for a reconstruction of society: and he wisely saw that true "reform" must not be separated from "Religion." "God is One," — he cried, again and again: and he urged that the Unity of God was the deepest utterance of Hindu Tradition.

The saints have taught that the One God has many "Names": and the saints have appeared in all countries and all ages. The saints have blessed the East and the West. The Buddha and Sri Ramakrishna, Mira and St. Francis, Kabir and Nanak, Rabia and Junnuna Misri, have, like other great mystics, pleaded for compassion, for sympathy, for self-abnegation, for communion with the poor.

Cast aside egoism, — has been the cry of all prophets and saints, St. Francis, Kabir and Ramakrishna, like other saints and *bhaktas,* sounded the note:— 'Renounce egotism and vanity!" Kabir, Nanak and St. Francis, like the Muslim mystics, Rabia and Junnuna Misri, were pictures of humility.

Sri Ramakrishna said, over and over again:— "God is the Inner Guide! He sees the longing of our hearts and the yearning of our souls!" And St. Mira, like St. Francis, moved from place to place, singing of love as the secret of Religion, —the secret of life in God. Life as we live it is, alas! A barrier between man and God. Life should be a Light, —like the sun that shines on all.

In a profound sense "pure knowledge," as Ramakrishna taught us, is blended with "pure love." God is Truth,— so taught the Rishis of the Upanishads. God is Love,—taught St. Francis and Kabir, Rabia and Junnuna Misri, St. Mira and Guru Nanak. It was a Tamil poet who sang:—

The Ignorant say that love and God are two,
But few do know the twain are one!
For love is God,
And whoso knoweth this
Rests in Love,— in God!

How compassionate was the Buddha! How loving have been the Saints! How patient was Rishi Dayanand! When persecuted, he retaliated not. When poisoned by his cook, whom some bribed to betray his master, the Rishi said:— "Dear Jagannath! here is money for your ticket: run immediately to another place: here you may be caught and tried and hanged to death." The truly great ones are always compassionate.

The nations, today are restless: and India, too, is swayed by storms. Yet is not "the world charged with the grandeur of God?" India and other nations need to listen to the voice of the prophets and saints:— "Man! thou art not a machine! Thou art divine! Within thee is a Light; let it shine in the midst of darkness and bear witness to Love as the Essence Pure of all that is!"

T. L. VASWANI.

Contents

Gautama Buddha: The Blessed One

The Holy Hermit

OVER FIVE AND twenty centuries ago was he born of Maharani Maya, "pure as a water-lily." His father, Suddhodana, was a king.

In the royal Lumbini grove, midway between Kapilavastu and Devadaha, Queen Maya brought forth her child, Gautama. Born of the royal family of the Sakyas, Gautama came to be called Sakyamuni (the *Muni* or Sage of the Sakya Community). He has been named, also, Siddhartha (he who achieved or attained the Goal). Yet another name given him is Tathagata, —one who "came in the same way," i.e. like the Buddhas before him. But the name by which he is known to millions of mankind is Buddha,— the "Enlightened One," the "Awakened One," the Master of Wisdom.

The royal father, radiant with joy, distributed alms among the poor and the helpless: and streets and bazars and houses and temples were decorated.

Asita was a *yogi*,— a holy hermit of the Himalayas, a grey-haired saint who lived near Kapilavastu. Wondrous was his knowledge of the Ancient Wisdom. He was a man of fasts and prayers. His ears heard, we read, in the hour of his meditation beneath the peepul-tree, the soges the Gods did sing at Buddha's birth. Asita came to see the new-born babe. The King saluted the *Yogi* and Queen Maya in reverence did lay her babe before his holy feet.

Holy Asita took the Prince in his arms, touched the dust and said:— "O Babe! I worship thee! Thou art Divine! In thee I see the Light such as never was on earth or sea! I see the marks on thy foot-sole, and I exclaim:— "Thou art the Buddha foretold of ancient times! Thou art the destined Preacher of the Law (*Dhamma*)! And thou art he who cometh to help and heal!"

Then, turning to the King, the Saint said:— "O King! but once in many myriad years doth appear in the Garden of Humanity a flower such as he,— a flower whose fragrance filleth the world from end to end."

Once again, Asita looked into Gautama's eyes, then sighed and wept.

"Why weepest thou, holy Hermit? Art thou not famed for wisdom and saintliness?" the King asked him.

And Asita answered thus:— "I weep, O King, because I shall not live to see the day that is to come, —the day when he, the Buddha, will teach the `Good Law' and bless the Nations of the Earth. I am old and I know my end is near!"

The Leela of His Life

On nine pictures have I loved to meditate, as I have dwelt in my mind on the life of the Buddha.

[1]

In the First Picture, we see Maharani Maya, the mother of Gautama. She is but forty-five years of age. It is the time of rain-festival in Kapilavastu. Queen Maya is asleep and is dreaming a dream. In her dream she sees a beautiful young elephant, white as milk, descending from Heaven. On waking up, Maharani May a feels that a Blessed One is coming. The white elephant is a symbol of gentleness. True it is, that Gautama was a picture of the gentle spirit. Gautama was a Teacher of Peace and Compassion.

[2]

In the Second Picture, we behold the birth of Gautama. He is born when his mother has reached the royal Park of Lumbini.

The Queen desires to have a little rest and so holds on to a branch of a Sal Tree, —when Gautama is born. All rejoice, for an heir is born to the house of Kapilavastu.

[3]

In the Third Picture, we see that Gautama, who is only sixteen years of age, marries Yashodhara, the beautiful daughter of the Koliyan King.

In the same Picture we see that Gautama lives a most comfortable life in three palaces specially built for him by his father. Maharaja Suddhodana has kept Gautama in ignorance of the seamy side of life. Gautama's movements are strictly guarded by a large number of servants whom the King has kept there, for he is afraid lest the prediction of the astrologers turn out true and Gautama, renouncing his home, becomes a mendicant and a wanderer. The thought of the Prince abandoning his home is a canker in the heart of the King and he is very careful, very watchful of every movement of Gautama, his beloved son.

[4]

In the Fourth Picture, we find Gautama moving out to see the city of his father. He sees Four Sights:— (i) an old man who feels very miserable; (ii) a sick man who, in pain and suffering, cries for help; (iii) a corpse; and (iv) a mendicant, an ascetic who has realised the vanity of the world. Gautama sees these Four Sights, realises that all men are subject to birth, decay, suffering and death, and he says to himself:— "What is life but one vast field of ugliness and decay, of tears and pain, of suffering and death!"

[5]

The next Picture is a very moving one. It is the Picture of Gautama's "Great Renunciation." Gautama decides to withdraw into silence and solitude and spend his time in meditation. He is anxious to answer the one question of existence:— Is there a way to liberation from pain or is man condemned forever to sorrow and suffering?

Gautama renounces the world and goes out in quest. He seeks

the Way of Salvation for all creatures. He leaves Yashodhara and Rahula, with tears in his eyes. He leaves his palace in the midnight hour. His dear charioteer, Channa, is by him. Gautama mounts his horse, Kanthaka, and rides for a long distance. He dismounts when the morning dawns. On the bank of the river Anoma stands Gautama. He puts off his princely robe and puts on the garb of a mendicant. He takes leave of Channa. With a brave heroic heart, Gautama goes into the Forest. Alone is he in that hour of dawn,— alone, yet strong in the faith that he will surely know Truth, one day, and find the Way of help and healing for the world's great sorrow.

[6]

In the nex Picture, we see Gautama blends his love for wisdom with self-control. He is prepared to submit to any ascetic self-denial, if only he will attain to Wisdom or Truth. For seven years he seeks, he struggles, he tries a number of experiments.

(1) He enquires of hermits and sages. Two of them are particularly mentioned in Buddhist books. One is named Alara Kalama: the other is Uddaka Ramaputta. Alara Kalama was a renowned philosopher of those days. Gautama joins this philosopher first, but is disappointed in his philosophy. He passes on next to Uddaka, but is soon disappointed in him, too.

(2) Gautama follows the method of breath-control. He can sit so still and motionless, that birds and beasts in the Forest do not feel disturbed by his presence. Gautama finds that this, too, has not induced that awakening or illumination which he is seeking. Breath-control, he begins to realise, is not control of consciousness.

(3) Later on, Gautama meets five brahmin ascetics who have been practising severe ascetic austerities. Gautama joins them and submits to severe ascetic disciplines. For six long years and more, he lives a life of intense mortification. He goes on reducing his food everyday. At last, he takes no more, — according to a statement attributed to him in the Buddhist books, — that one grain of rice a day. Gautama is reduced to a skeleton. The five brahmin ascetics admire Gautama's ascetic life and become his disciples.

One day, he swoons in utter exhaustion. For many hours he lies unconscious. He wakes up and realises that such severe asceticism results in *exhaustion*, not *illumination*, in impotence of the mind, not in the peace which he is seeking. On waking up, Gautama feels he must follow a different method. Extreme asceticism, he feels leads to torpor, not to wakefulness.

What is Gautama to do now? No philosopher and no ascetic teacher comes to his help. Breath-control has not helped him. He has tried, also, the method of silence. For a long time he has not spoken to any man. But this, too, has not proved fruitful. The only result he can see is that he is become very weak. "Thin and lean," Gautama said at a later stage, "thin and lean as a reed did my arms and legs become. I was no nearer to knowledge or illumination!"

Gautama now makes up his mind to eat a little. He goes to a village in search of nourishment. His five brahmin disciples now lose their faith in him. For Gautama has departed from extreme asceticism: he has taken a little food. The five companions of Gautama feel scandalised, because he has given up mortifications as exhausting and useless. Yes, — Gautama has given up the ascetic denial of the demands of the body.

At this stage it is, that Sujata appears. It is the day before the full-moon day of Vaisakh. Gautama is sitting at the foot of a tree, waiting for the hour when he is to go out, taking his bowl to beg his food. Sujata is the daughter of a rich headman who lives in a village near Uruvala. Sujata has prepared milk-rice and has placed it in a golden bowl. She sees Gautama sitting beneath a tree. "Verily, a God is here," she says. And she places the golden bowl of milk-rice in Gautama's hands.

Gautama accepts Sujata's offering and blesses her. Gautama eats the food. Then he sets the bowl floating on the river, saying:— "If, today, I am abie to become a Buddha, let this bowl go up the stream, if not, let the bowl go down the stream!" And the Buddhist tradition has it that the bowl went up.

[7]

Gautama has now moved on to a big peepul-tree. Under the shade of this Tree, Gautama is destined to find what he seeks. The Tree is destined to become the Wisdom-Tree, the Bodhi-Tree. Absorbed in concentration, underneath the Bodhi-Tree, Gautama realises the cause of suffering and its destruction. He realises the Four Noble Truths:— (1) suffering; (2) cause of suffering; (3) removal of suffering; and (4) the Way which one may tread for removal of suffering. Gautama attains to *nirvana*. He has become Buddha.

In the evening, as he is sitting beneath the Bodhi-Tree, we see that Mara, the Dark One, advances with his army to assail Gautama. Mara cannot prevail. For Gautama, indeed, has passed beyond the cycle of re-birth. Mara is deeply distressed at the heights which Gautama has attained. Mara tempts Buddha with all the strength which Dark Powers can wield.

According to the Buddhist tradition, a huge army stands by Mara. They all invade the Blessed One. Single is he, but his strength is the strength of millions. Mara attacks the Buddha with arrows first, then with pieces of rock. Then Mara stirs up a storm of wind. Then with blazing weapons, darts of burning flame, is the Buddha assailed. But every arrow, every piece of rock, and storms of wind and rain, and every dart of the burning flame fall gently on the Buddha: for all are changed into garlands of flowers. And round the Blessed One appears a halo of light.

Then Mara tells Gautama:— " You have attained. Why think you now of mankind? How many to whom you speak will understand you? Be absorbed in you own joy, — of *nirvana*! Leave mankind in ignorance and sin. They will not respond to you."

Then to Mara says Buddha, — serene and motionless, sitting on his seat with the composure of a sage:— "I will not listen to thee, Mara! Wisdom hath come to me that I may share it with mankind, for men are in suffering and pain. And I must go forth to preach enlightenment and the Way to a world which, alas! is in darkness and woe!"

Then says Mara to Gautama:— "Get up from thy seat! It belongs to me, not to you!"

But Gautama sits unruffled, saying to Mara:— "Who is your witness?"

And the hosts of Mara shriek:— "We bear witness! We bear witness!"

Then Mara asks Gautama:— "Who is your witness?"

with his right hand, we read, Gautama touches the earth and says:— "The Earth is my witness!"

Then disappear Mara's army as illusory forms. And Mara himself falls on his knees.

So true it is, that the Earth, the wide, spacious Earth, the whole world bears witness to the Wisdom of the Buddha and the Saints. While the powers of darkness can but appear for sometime in forms which prove illusory, they cannot abide: for they are born of illusion *maya*.

Gautama has conquered Mara. The story is, to my mind, very suggestive, because it is symbolic of a great spiritual truth. Mara's full name is Kama-Mara. "*Kama*" means "desire," "*Mara*" means "death." Desire and death are, indeed, masters of the world-illusion to which the majority of men are subject. Desire and death, *kama-mara*, the Buddha overcame, as always the truly wise ones conquer the powers of darkness.

And Buddha, overcoming the tempter, remains in meditation, in *dhyana*, experiencing the joy of the great Awakening. Untouched, the Buddha remains beneath the Bo-Tree. And he became, the Buddhist tradition tells us, the triple Teacher:— (1) the Teacher of men; (2) the Teacher of the Gods; and (3) the Teacher of the created world. Buddha became the Great Teacher: for indeed, men and Gods and all creatures move in a world of sleep, and Buddha came to awaken them from their deep slumber.

[8]

Buddha now moves out to different places, interpreting his message to crowds of men and healing many hearts.

(1) He announces his message first to the five brahmin ascetics who were once his disciples but who had deserted him. He moves on in search of them, untill he comes to Sarnath (near Banaras), where he gives his First Discourse.

(2) He comes next to the kingdom of Magadha and preaches to King Bimbisara: the King becomes a disciple and recites the

words:— "I take refuge in the Buddha! I take refuge in the Dhamma! I take refuge in the Sangha!" The King dedicates his spacious garden, called Veluvana, to the Brotherhood.

(3) The Buddha proceeds to Sravasti. There lives a very wealthy man named Anathapindika. He hears the Buddha and dedicates his life to the Lord. Anathapindika decides to give a donation to the Sangha. He asks Prince Jeta for his beautiful grove. The Prince is not inclined to sell it and says:— "If thou canst cover the ground with gold, thou mayst have it." The Prince then learns that Anathapindika wants to build and *asrama* there for the Sangha: the prince joyfully agrees to accept only half the price. So is the *asrama* built in the grove and dedicated to Buddha and his Order.

(4) The Buddha not only preaches: he, also, serves. For he is not only the Teacher: he is, also, the Compassionate One. He learns of an old *bhikkhu* suffering from a loathsome skin disease. The *bhikkhu* cannot get up from his bed: he lies there helpless: for no one comes near him. The Buddha goes to the *bhikkhu's* chamber, pours warm water over the sick *bhikkhu*, and speaks the moving words:—

"Brethren!
He who serveth the sick,—
Verily, he serveth me!"

(5) The Buddha comes to the Banyan-grove near Kapilavastu. There he learns that there is a dispute between the Sakyas and the Koliyas with regard to the water of the river Rohini. The water has not sufficed to irrigate the rice-fields of both the Sakyas and the Koliyas. The dispute threatens to develop into a war. Buddha proceeds to the spot to reconcile the two parties. He hears them both. He gives a discourse pointing out that a war would do harm to both. In peace, he points out, is the gain of both. The Sakyas and the Koliyas are reconciled.

(6) Buddha's father, Maharaja Suddhodana, learns that Buddha is near Kapilavastu. With his relatives and ministers and some townsmen, women and children, the Maharaja goes forth to invite his son to the palace. There the Buddha speaks to the Maharaja

and the Sakyas, saying:— "Seven years have passed since I left you. I come back to you, bringing to you a gift more precious than the richest treasure of the earth, —the gift of the Eightfold Way."

The Maharaja and yashodhara and her son Rahula and many nobles of Kapila are converted to the Buddhist Brotherhood.

(7) Buddha converts the dacoit and murderer, Angulimala, who wears a wreath of the nine hundred and ninety-nine fingers of the men he has murdered. The robber needs one more finger to fulfil his vow. Seeing the Buddha, the dacoit says:— "Him shall I kill to complete a wreath of a thousand fingers." The dacoit with a sword in his hand goes forth to kill Gautama: he runs and runs but cannot catch the Buddha. Then cries out Angulimala:— "Stand still, O Samana! Stand still, O Samana!" Straight comes the gentle reply of the Buddha:—

"I am still!
Be thou, too, still!"

Then the Buddha explains what real stillness means: and Buddha tranquillises the heart of Angulimala and wins him over to the Dhamma. Angulimala falls at the Buddha's feet and asks to be forgiven. Angulimala weeps and says:— "Master! I take refuge at thy feet!" And Buddha receives him into the Brotherhood.

(8) The Blessed One moves from village to village, bringing peace to many a saddened heart and speaking to multitudes of the Way of Deliverance and Peace.

[9]

The last scene in the earth-life of the Blessed One is most moving. And the Picture of the passing of the Buddha has, again and again, moved my eyes to tears.

The Buddha is in the Sala grove of the Mallas of Kusinara, Between two Sala trees, with his head to the North, the Buddha lies down ready to depart and pass into *Mahanirvana*. Ananda, with tears in his eyes, goes to the city to tell the mallas:— "The Master says he will pass away tonight!"

The Mallas come with their wives and children and bow to the

Blessed One and weep bitterly. He speaks to them:— "Weep not! All component things are subject to decay." The Buddha speaks, also, to Ananda and the *bhikkhus*. Then is uttered the last word of the Buddha:— "Brethren! work out your salvation with diligence!"

In The Forest

At the age of twenty-nine, Gautama goes out to see the city of his father. He sees an old man, then a sick man, then a dead body. These three sights rouse an agitation in his heart. But this agitation is not yet become a feeling of renunciation. When he sees the fourth sight, —an ascetic in a yellow garb, a man of utter poverty and renunciation but with serenity on his face, —there dawns on him a "Recollection" and he realises that all beings and all forms of life in the *sansara* (the world) are subject to birth, decay, suffering and death.

As he passes through the city, on his way back to the palace, a maiden sees him and in joy she utters the words which enter deep into Gautama's heart and strengthen his resolve of renunciation. This girl utters the following words:—

"Verily, happy (*nibbuta*) is his mother!
Verily, happy (*nibbuta*) is his father!
Verily, happy (*nibbuta*) is the wife,
Who has such a husband as he!"

Gautama hears the words and reflects on them. The word, *nibbuta*, specially, strikes his imagination. The word has a double meaning: it means (1) "happy" and (2) "extinguished". Yes,— Gautama says to himself on his way to the palace, — he is truly happy who hath "extinguished" fires.

"When the fire of passion is extinguished, the heart is happy!
When the fire of hate is extinguished, the heart is happy!
When the fire of pride is extinguished, the heart is happy!

Filled with the thought that the road to happiness is extinguishing of fires, — the fires of passion and hate and pride, — Gautama returns to his palace. But before he reaches it, he sends that girl a necklace of precious pearls with the words:— "You, O blessed one! have taught me the very first lession in spiritual life. And I send you as my *bheta*, an offering, this necklace. May you accept it!"

Gautama returns to his palace. His father sends him the message:— "A son, my son! is born to thee."

As his answer to his father's news, he says:— "Rahula is born! A fetter is born!" For the word "rahula" *means* "fetter."

The words of Gautama are conveyed to the King. And Rahula becomes the name of Gautama's son.

The night has now arrived. And Gautama continues to reflect on the Way to Happiness. Again and again, he says to himself:— "Fires! Fires! Put out the fires if you will be truly happy!"

The night is advancing. Gautama is still awake. In the middle of the night, he says to himself:—"I must leave this palace and go out into the darkness of the Great Unknown, and in that darkness find the Light of my life."

Gautama would fain look at his son before leaving the palace. But he fears to awaken yashodhara. She is asleep. He goes on tiptoe to get his son's blessings. But Rahula is asleep with his mother. He gazes at both. Tears touch his eyes: he turns away: he leaves in silence.

Channa, his charioteer, is with him. Gautama mounts his white horse, Kanthaka. Quick he crosses the country. He reaches the river.—Anoma.

And now comes the parting moment. To Channa, Gautama gives his perfumed clothing and all his precious ornaments, the rings and the necklace. To Channa, too, Gautama gives his beloved horse, Kanthaka, saying:— "Take care of Kanthaka who hath always blessed me."

Then Gautama, putting off his clothing, wears Channa's cloak, — a poor man's cloak. Gautama has joined the noblest brotherhood of all, — the brotherhood of the poor.

One more act inspired by the spirit of renunciation. Gautama has parted with good clothes and ornaments. Gautama must, also, part with his beauty. With strokes of his sabre, he cuts off his hair and his beard.

And now, thanking Channa for all his services, Gautama says:— "Brother Channa! go now and bless me!"

Gautama now receives the eight requisites of a monk, namely, three robes, bowl, razor, needle, girdle and water-strainer. Whence does he get them? From a *fakir* or from some other source, I know not. But this, I believe, may well be accepted that Gautama goes on to the Rajagriha with the requisites of a monk.

The King of the place was Bimbisara. Rajagriha: the name is significant. Raja-griha: "griha" means "the dwelling-place," "city." Rajagriha means "the city of kings." In that city was a cave: it may still be seen. And peasants of the countryside today call it the "Sonar Bhandar," the Golden Treasury,— whereby runs a story known to the village-folk. For they, some of them, still believe that the Cave, —Sonar Bhandar, —is filled with grains of gold. But the Cave will not open except to the touch of the Buddha who, they believe, will come again and, opening the Cave, will distribute grains of gold among the poor, hungry village-folk. In this Cave, it is believed, Gautama spent sometime in meditation.

Rajagriha was, doubtless, a beautiful place. A Chinese pilgrim, in his description of Rajagriha, speaks of it as the place where peacocks were fed.

Bimbisara comes to know that Gautama has journeyed to Rajagriha,—Gautama, the Sakya Prince, the beloved son of Raja Suddhodana. Bimbisara has heard that Gautama has renounced royalty to become a *fakir* and is in quest of the meaning of life. Raja Bimbisara goes forth to meet Gautama. Raja Bimbisara offers half his kingdom to Gautama. But who can tempt a true *fakir* with offers of wealth or kingdom? Gautama hath renounced them. A beautiful smile still plays upon his lips. And, in answer to Raja Bimbisara's offer, Gautama says:— "This life, O King! is a life of bondage. This life is pain. Free only is he who lives, not in a palace, but in the open air of the Forest. To the Forest let me go!"

Scholars have raised the question, why Gautama came all the way to Rajagriha. In the neighbourhood of Rajagriha, from time to time, were held conferences of scholars and learned men. What had Gautama to do with them? Gautama sought a treasure richer by far than any treasure of learning or scholarship, metaphysics or philosophy. Gautama sought the treasure of that wisdom which is not in books or scriptures, but which is in the illumined mind. Gautama, doubtless, came to Rajagriha, feeling that in the solitude of the Forest there, he would be far from the crowds of men and would sit in silence to assimilate the wisdom of nature and, in brooding thought, to lift his consciousness to a realisation of the meaning of life. Gautama came to Rajagriha in search of truth and wisdom.

On The Vaisakhi Night

Days pass into months and months into years. It is the seventh year of Gautama's renunciation.

Living in the Forest, Gautama thinks, again and again, of the sufferings of men. He lives on wild fruit fallen from the trees. For days together, he starves. His body has lost the beauty of youth. Gautama, once the flower of all his land, looks now lean and pale.

One day, there passes by the road a band of girls. They are moving on to a temple in the town. One of them is beating a drum. Another is playing on a flute. A third girl is twitching a three-stringed *sitar.* On the *sitar* she sings:—

> Fair, indeed, doth the dancing go
> When the *sitar* is tuned aright!
> This, indeed, I know
> That we must tune the *sitar*
> Neither low nor high!
> So may we win the hearts of men.
> For the string overstretched doth break.
> And music flies!
> But the string overslack is dumb,

And music dies!
So I sing:—
Tune the *sitar* neither low nor high!

And the words fall on Gautama's ears as he sits under the peepul-tree by the path.

And Gautama lifts his brow and says:—

The foolish sometimes teach the wise.
I truly strain too much
The strings of the *sitar.*
My eyes are dim,
My strength is waned,
My need is great.
And now I know,
If I continue thus to strain
The string of life,
I shall die:
And then must die, too,
All hope of finding the Way
Out of the world's great sorrow
To Deliverance and Peace!

Gautama has now mentally abandoned the severe ascetic discipline which has so weakened him that his body is become almost a reed.

It is the day before the full-moon day of the holy month of Vaisakh. Gautama is sitting at the foot of a peepul-tree. A Village-girl walks in, —singing. Her name is Sujata. She is the daughter of a rich headman who lives in a village, near Uruvala. What a moving song she sings!

I walk in the meadows:
I look at the flowers:
I listen to their song!
Are they flowers or poems pure
The Maker of stars and the earth,
The Maker of worlds and of men
Breathes forth in beauty of the Dawn?

How happy I feel!
Filled am I with joy supreme,
All day and all night!
For He, the Maker of heaven and earth,—
He loveth me,
And I love Him,
As I gaze into the myriad stars
That look on this earth
With love-lit eyes
From Beauty's Realm,
Far, far away!

Sujata had vowed to offer milk-rice in a golden bowl to the Tree-God that day. Sujata sees Gautama sitting beneath the Tree and is filled with joy. "Verily," she says, "the Tree-God is here: how he shines!"

She bows down to him and places the dish of milk-rice in his hands. Gautama accepts the offering and blesses her. Sujata wonders how the Holy One knows her!

Gautama is grateful to her for her milk-rice. He will now have the strength to walk to an old, old peepul-tree. "There shall I sit," he says to himself; "perhaps, I shall find the Truth,—at last!"

Gautama walks to the Tree. He sits at the foot of the Tree on a handful of grass. Eight handfuls of grass a gardener has given him for his seat. From the rising to the setting of the sun, Gautama sits there, meditating on Life, on Suffering, on its cause and cure. Underneath the old, old Tree he sits, his breathing so quiet and so rhythmic that the little creatures that are nearby look at him and are unafraid. He now hath found the true key to wisdom,—meditation and communion with the Silence within.

Gautama, in his meditation, begins to understand that emancipation, *moksha*, is (1) not won by mortification, (2) but neither is it an intellectual process or a philosophic thing.

Emancipation, he realises, is a result of long discipline, of *sadhanas*. It is a new birth. Emancipation is liberation from attachment to *trisna*, craving, desire,—attachment to the false self. *Trisna* binds us to the body and is, therefore, a source of separation. He who is purged of *trisna* is purified at once in the mind and the heart. He enters into the Highest which Buddha names *nirvana.* Not through the intellect may you be led to the Highest.

At last has Buddha awakened from the dream of the senses. And on the Vaisakhi Day, he goes into the Trance and in it he beholds the Chain of Cause and Effect. He beholds, too, the Path of Deliverance into Peace and Joy.

In the Trance, Gautama attains to Knowledge, Enlightenment. He realises that (1) nothing is permanent: all things change: all things pass away: the very mountains are not "*achala*," immovable, but are as "clouds of dust."

(2) The "ego" we call "I" doth also change like the colours of sunrise: the "ego" is "nothing": "we" are nothing: we but move in a scene of continuous Becoming.

(3) A chain of cause and effect is our "empirical" life: and the chain is not snapped by death.

(4) The great illusion of life is the feeling of "separateness." "I" am "they": "they" are "I." I am one with them, one with all,—one with birds and beasts, one with insects and trees, one with the earth, one with the stars one with the suns and worlds in space!

(5) In "separateness" is the world's great misery: in "compassion" (*maitri*) is the world's true strength. "Peace" doth not "pass" understanding: "peace" lies in "understanding," in Wisdom, in the Perception that Life is One and that I should touch Life in sympathy and compassion, recognising that in all the million forms and changes migrates but One Life. The illusion of "separateness" must go. In this illusion is the seed of desire. Therefore, the desire, to crave, is to suffer. Nothing that you "desire" can ever give you peace: for nothing that you desire can ever endure. *Trisna*, appetite, craving, is a feeling for the changing, the passing, the impermanent and can never draw you near to Peace and Happiness.

Buddha, I may be permitted to say, has risen beyond the "mind," the "mental body." Buddha has realised that the cosmic energy has put an upward reach into the consciousness of man. Buddha has passed into contemplation. He has entered into ecstasy. He now hath seen that the builder of the prison, which we call the body, is *trisna*. This false self, the ego, is the cause of re-birth. This ego is the source of desires and, therefore, of illusions: it is the dreamer of dreams. It is Schopenhauer's the "will-to-live." This ego is dead in Gautama: and he is become a victor.

The Tree, under which Gautama, sitting in meditation, awoke to Enlightenment, is held in the highest veneration by the Buddhists. They rightly speak of it as the "Sacred Bodhi Tree," the Sacred Tree of Knowledge. The Tree has been re-planted from its own seeds, again and again: you may see it, today, at Buddha-Gaya. The Illumination which entered Gautama's heart occurred, we are told at the full-moon of May, in the year 544 B.C. We celebrate, this year, in different parts of the world, the 2500th anniversary of that event.

In his illumined consciousness, Buddha seized the very secret of desire or *trisna*. Desire is restlessness of wants. Therefore is desire insatiable. It belongs to the domain of the "mind." But to a higher domain belongs the Peace which Gautama attained, at last. It is the domain of the purified heart, the purified will and the purified understanding. In this triple synthesis is the secret of *bodhi*.

Many in the modern world see behind history only economic forces. But behind these forces, I humbly submit, and at the summit of a truly vital civilisation, stand as guides and pioneers those truly great ones who have transcended the mind and become voices and interpreters of the *buddhi*,—the purified heart, the purified will, the purified understanding. In this vision, perceived by the *buddhi*, of the One Life, all forms are seen as passing, all forms are *anatta*. The Buddhist doctrine of *anatta*, I interpret, not as a doctrine of non-existence of the Supreme or the Spirit, but as a doctrine which affirms that while all forms perish, Life persists, the Spirit endures.

Prince Gautama is now become Buddha, enlightened. He now knows. False desires die. No longer is he a prisoner of the sense. We hath he been compared to a "lamp that shineth in a windless place and flickereth not". "I have attained!" the Buddha saith.

With the Vision of the Secret of Life, Buddha experiences peace, infinite peace in his heart. Buddha, also, has another experience.—that of compassion. In his heart wells up infinite compassion for the toiling, unhappy millions of mankind and for all creatures groaning in agony and pain. Buddha is filled with pity towards the entire creation. A flood of light fills his heart. He sees the Way. He sees, too, the steps, the eight steps to reach the Goal. And he realises that the Way is not meant for a few, a chosen class or sect, a select caste segregated from humanity. The Way, Buddha sees, is within the reach of all who will walk, step by step, in love and patience.

In his Vision he sees what are the causes of suffering. He sees that human life is a chain.

(1) The first link in the chain is contact (*sparsham*),—contact with matter. Contact produces sensation.

(2) Out of sensation awakes desire, *tanha, trisna.*

(3) Out of desire or *tanha* springs attachment to the shows and illusions of life.

(4) Out of attachment is born *karma*, action, deed.

(5) Out of *karma* is birth.

(6) Out of birth are age, sickness and death,—springs of suffering.

Gautama, becoming the Buddha, is filled with joy. And the Buddhist books tell us that in joy he utters the following:—

Many a house of life,
Through many a round
Of many births,
Had held me!
How painful, O, is birth,
Again and Again! O thou,
The builder of the body-prison!
I behold thee now.
Thou shalt not build again!
These walls of pain,
These rafters of clay
Are broken now!
The ridge-pole is destroyed, too!
All cravings now are gone!

Beyond the mind
I have the *bodhi* reached:
I have at last attained!

This *bodhi* is *gnana*, is wisdom. It is necessary to remember that this wisdom is not a matter of books or scriptures. It is the wisdom of life: it is the wisdom that lifts us above experience to what Buddha repeatedly refers to as *maitri*, compassion. It is the wisdom of the Other Shore. The wisdom of compassion never cometh except in the measure in which we have learnt to renounce the "ego". This wisdom of the Other Shore is transmutation of life. This transmutation is release from the bondage of the ego and its desires, of the ego and its propensities, its cravings for the sensuous. When this transmutation takes place, a new realm is opened to us, a new outlook is developed. We are transformed, transmuted.

Compassion is essential to this "transmutation." We grow then in the feeling that we are not separate from creation. This truth is the vision of the one Buddha in all. Then we see the Buddha in the criminal and the animal, in the angel and the ant, in the sinner and the saint. This vision is compassion.

The Noble Teaching of the Buddha I can interpret in no better words than these:— Your life is fulfilled in meditation, compassion and service.

The great Vaisakhi vision which came to Buddha, I interpret thus:—Share and be selfless! In *maitri* or true "friendship" be linked with the poor and lowly! In compassion and love discover the meaning of life! If you would truly love, serve without stint or spare. Look at the sun! Even as it loveth us,—the poor no less than the rich, the sinner no less than the saint,—giving his radiance to all, even so love ye one another!

Devadatta plotted against Buddha and, in order to harm him, Devadatta sent to Buddha a fierce elephant. Buddha was compassionate. He charged the elephant with currents of compassion and love, and the elephant was subdued.

A story which has moved me much is a beautiful commentary on Buddha's compassion for animals. Buddha is in Rajagriha and is, one day, having a walk. He gazes at the beauty of the flowers of the field an says:— "O trees and flowers of the field! how trustfully your turn your faces to the sun! And how trustfully nightingales and doves take shelter in you! Alas! man hurts the birds and slays the animals! The wisdom of man is drenched in blood!"

Just then, a flock of goats and sheep passes by. Buddha finds that the herdsman is driving them with difficulty.

"What is the matter?" asks Buddha.

The herdsman says:— "Sir! there is in the herd a limping lamb. He finds it difficult to keep pace with others in the herd."

Affectionately, Buddha takes the limping lamb on his shoulder.

Then, Buddha asks the herdsman:— "Why are you driving the herd in the heat of the noon-day sun?"

The herdsman says:—"I am asked to give the King a hundred goats and sheep for sacrifice in the *yagna* which takes place this evening."

And Buddha says:—"I, too, shall go!"

They enter the city, side by side,—the herdsman and Gautama. Meekly walks Gautama with the lamb on his shoulder. They cross the bazar. And the buyers in the market stop awhile to gaze at Gautama. And women open their doors to see how gently and gracefully he walks,—this great lover of peace! He moves on. Many gaze at him, again and again. Many know him not. They have but heard of him and say:—"Behold the holy man who dwells on the Hill!"

And Buddha reaches the place where preparations have been made for sacrifice in the *yagna*. The man in charge is about to strike the sword against the goat marked for sacrifice, when suddenly Buddha exclaims:—"Great King! let not the man strike! Take my life as a sacrifice, O King! and spare the lamb."

The words move the heart of the King. He, then, asks Gautama to speak to the people. A few words only does Gautama speak on the occasion:—

> O men! you can take life easily but, remember, none of you can give life!
>
> So, have mercy, have compassion makes the world noble

and beautiful.

Remember, too, that all living beings are linked together in *maitri*.

Therefore, resolve that you will live on bloodless diet. Verily, in gentleness is the crown of life!

The next day, a decree is proclaimed by the King. The order goes forth that none shall henceforth kill for sacrifice or for private pleasure. For Life is one: and the crown of life is mercy of compassion.

Blessed Are They Who Walk The Way

"Among the people must I go!" says Buddha. "They suffer and I must speak to them of the Way to Peace and Joy."

To Sarnath, he comes to meet, if he can, the five *bhikkhus* who had been with him for sometime but who had left him when he gave up the ascetic way. The ascetic way, he had come to realise, was not the heroic way. The five ascetics see him at a distance, and they say:— "Here comes a renegade: we will show him no respect!"

Gautama draws nearer: they see him and are wonder-struck. A mysterious force seems to go out of him: they cannot resist it! One of them quickly prepares a seat for him: another holds in his hands the begging bowl of the Buddha: the third ascetic brings water to wash the feet of the Blessed One!

The Buddha gives his first sermon to the five *bhikkhus*: and they become his disciples again. Buddha's "Sermon at Sarnath" is well named the "Turning to the Wheel." The Buddha "turns" at Sarnath the Wheel of *Dharma*, pointing out that the universe moves round the "Wheel of Law."

In this "Sermon at Sarnath," the Buddha gives the essence of his Teaching. He calls it the "Message of the Middle Way." In Buddha's days, some followed the "ascetic way." Some others followed the "way of pleasure (*bhoga*)." Buddha said:—The right way is neither the way of pleasure nor the way of asceticism. The right way is the heroic way,—the way of self-control, the way of purity and restraint.

Buddha emphasises the four "Aryan" Truths, the four Noble Truths. These "Truths" may briefly be summed up thus:—

(1) Suffering is a fact. To be born is to suffer. To live is to suffer. From birth to death thou dost suffer, O man!

(2) Back of suffering is ignorance, ignorant craving or *tanha*, the illusion of "I," the false "self." In this illusion of the "ego" doth man wander from birth to birth. In ignorance he moves on, unhappy, a victim to "thirst," *trisna*. Threefold is this thirst:— (i) there is the thirst due to lust of flesh; (ii) there is the thirst due to lust of the eyes; and (iii) there is the thirst due to pride of life.

(3) The cure of thirst is extinction of *trisna*, letting it go! Expel desire! Renouce attachment! In "desire," you "separate" yourself from others: in desire you become a creature of the body. This "separateness" will (i) if you learn discipline,—the discipline of will-power; and (ii) if in your heart is awakened compassion for all creatures,—for men and birds and beasts. "Compassion" is "*maitri*." Filled with *maitri*, compassion, be one with the One Life.

(4) The way to extinguish desire, *trisna*, is the Eightfold Path, —the Path which has "Eight Noble Steps" aiming at awakening of *maitri* and compassion in the heart.

These "Four Noble Truths" are beautifully expounded by Buddha in the following words:—

(1) Now this, O monks, is the noble truth of pain: birth is painful, sickness is painful, old age is painful, sorrow, lamentation, dejection and desire are painful.

(2) Now this, O monks, is the noble truth of the *cause of pain*. The cause is the craving which leads to re-birth, combined with pleasure and lust, finding pleasure here and there, namely, the craving for passion, the craving for existence, the craving for non-existence.

(3) Now this, O monks, is the noble truth of the *cessation of pain*,— the cessation, without a remainder, of that craving: abandonment, forsaking, release, *non-attachment*.

(4) Now this, O monks, is the noble truth of the Way that leads to the cessation of pain. This is the Noble Eightfold Way, namely, right views, right intention, right speech, right action, right living, right effort, right mindfulness, right concentration.

The Path, the Noble Path, the "Eightfold Path" has the following "eight steps" to "Knowledge" called *Bodhi* (Illumination). Light shines in him who treads the Path, step by step.

I. The very first step is right understanding, right view or comprehension. Right view is his who does not mistake the passing for the Abiding, the transient for the Permanent. Wrong views, doubts, mere "opinions," must be laid aside.

(1) Right understanding is his who does not fall into error: and the greatest error is his who regards "ego" as the "Reality." The "ego" is "illusion." In the journey through *sansara* (the world) to Liberation, the illusion of the "ego" must be shed.

(2) Realise, therefore, that you move in a transient world. Nothing that you see is Permanent: for nothing that "separates" is permanent. What "separates" is the "body," the "ego." What "separates" is "illusion." For Life is One. Forms are transient: Life, the One Life, is permanent and moves on!

II. The second step in the Path is right resolution, right intention and aspiration, right purpose. This is the will-to-attain based on (1) self-discipline and (2) the vision that Knowledge or Illumination is possible. In this world of suffering, intend, aspire, resolve that you will lessen suffering, not increase it. Develop will-power. Resolve that you will attain to Knowledge or Illumination which will lead you out of suffering. Through self-discipline you can attain to Knowledge.

The second step, then, in the Path,—the step of right resolve,—is taken by him (1) who has no desire to harm any living creature; and (2) who strives to free himself from the slavery of the senses.

III. The third step is right speech. This is the *first* step in the *practice* of self-discipline. Right speech is essential to self-discipline. Right speech is his (1) who does not speak untruth; (2) who does away with indiscretion, slander, abuse, bitter words; (3) who speaks gently to all, who is not cruel in words, who never speaks in anger of malice: his words are kind and pure; and (4) who speaks neither in self-glorification nor in hate. Such a man speaks in sympathy, knowing that suffering surrounds us all.

IV. The fourth step is right conduct.

(1) He acts rightly who puts away all thought of gain or reward, here or hereafter.

(2) He acts impersonally. It is not enought to have the right appearance: you act rightly when your *inner* motive is right. The motive is the deed. Such a man eliminates all thought of retaliation.

(3) His conduct is guided by the Inward Law, the *Dharma*, the Moral Law. He realises the truth of the injunctions:— "Thou shalt not kill!" "Thou shalt not commit adultery!"

(4) Continuing to act according to Law, he finds, one day, that he has developed *insight*. When his deeds are in harmony with and not out of the Moral Law, he developes *insight* into life, and he realises that the purpose of life is not power but blessedness, joy, peace!

V. The fifth step is right means of livelihood, "Right" means "ethical". Maintain your integrity and purity. This is the moral foundation of life.

(1) He who takes step number five in the Path earns his livelihood honestly. He realises that in his work he must be honest. He avoids taking bribes: he avoids, too, taking undue advantage of another. "Thou shalt not rob",—is one of the injunctions of Buddha. He, also, says:— "Thou shalt not drink alcoholic liquors." Right conduct, thus, must be enriched by right living.

(2) Such a man is blessed, indeed: he is not a *doubter*. and he *acts* with a clear mind. His *anna* (food) being pure, his *mana* (mind), too, becomes pure.

VI. The sixth step is right use of energy, right effort. Right use of energy is use in *obedience* to Law.

(1) Such a man eats, drinks, sleeps, works, rests,—in accordance with Law, the *Dhamma*.

(2) Therefore, he does not waste his energy in spectacles of idle dancing or singing which do not uplift but only distract.

VII. The seventh step is right mindfulness, right alertness, awareness, watchfulness. His mind strives for peace. He aims at Truth. The man who moves on the Path, in the seventh step, is aware that life is sacred. He keeps awake,—day and night. He is ever watchful lest he fall. The great Truths of Life are ever before him—a light on the path of life.

VIII. The eighth step is right concentration or meditation. For this self-control is necessary. The meditative man is a man of self-control. He radiates sympathy and love. He becomes a man of *maitri,* compassion. He sees himself as a part of the Whole, the Infinite, and he learns to love,—not his separate life, but all men, all living beings.

Life, it is true, is to be purified. But purification is through compassion. You must throw away the idols of false and conventional life. Hence the importance of meditation. This will give you new insight, new knowledge. When compassion is born in you, you gather new strength to serve the world. Buddha holds that there is something wrong with the universe: nature and man contain something blind, petrified, dead: we live in a cosmic cemetery. The universe we see around us is a "false" universe. Yet through meditation and contemplation the earth may become a mirror of the Divine.

Treading this Path,—the Eightfold Path,—the mortal may attain to the Perfect Life which Buddha referred to, again and again, as *Nirvana* (Peace). This Path is the Path to Liberation: it is not the Path of rites and ceremonies. It is the Path of virtue and sanctity. What you need is the *will* for right thought and right action (*karma*), the will for virtue and purification.

This "Noble Eightfold Path" may well be presented in the form of the following eight beatitudes:—

[1]

Blessed are they who understand
That Life is One.
Its "forms" do come and go:
But Life itself floweth on!

[2]

Blessed are they who resolve
That they will build the strength
To lessen suffering and pain
And attain to wisdom pure!

[3]

Blessed are they who speak
In sympathy and gently to all,
Who do away with bitter words
And never speak in anger or in hate!

[4]

Blessed are they who rightly act
And put away all thought of gain,
Who know that motive is the deed
And who, renouncing power, are pure, indeed!

[5]

Blessed are they who earn
Their daily bread in such a way
That brings not hurt nor pain
To living creatures on the Earth!

[6]

Blessed are they who cast
Out ill-will and pride in daily life
And act obedient to the Law
In sympathy and love!

[7]

Blessed are they who walk the Way,
Aware by night and day that life is sacred still!
They strive for Peace: and ever before them shine
The noble Truths of life!

[8]

Blessed are they who meditate
In silent joy and see how rich, indeed,
Is the life of Compassion, Service, Love!
Radiant as the Lamp of Light is such a life.

Thus taught the Blessed One, moving from town to town and village to village, teaching men and women the Way of Deliverance,—the Way of Peace, Compassion and Illumination.

Three Baskets

In the world's history, ancient or modern, there has not appeared another who received in his own life-time the reverent homage of millions as Buddha did. Buddha impressed his will on the people. India under his influence became, practically, a vegetarian country. For five hundred years and more, the governing principle of India's life was *Daya Dharma* (The Religion of Compassion).

Yet let us not think that Buddha did his work without opposition. It was no path of roses Buddha trod. In the early period of his ministry, he was abused, opposed, persecuted. He conquered by love. Buddha, said his opponents, was a thief, because he had "destroyed faith in animal sacrifices"! "Do not see even his face,"—said they about him. One day, he could not get even a morsel of food as alms in a village! Sonadanda was a learned brahmin. He was advised, for the sake of his reputation among men, not to see Buddha!

Sundąri was a nun. Buddha's persecutors hired some bad men to kill her. Her body was thrown into a thicket near the monastery where Buddha was staying. "Gautama," said his opponents, "is the author of the crime." Gautama was quiet, patient, and forgiving. One day, the real assassins got drunk and, in a drunken state, revealed the conspiracy. So the real culprits were found, and Buddha's enemies were put to shame.

Cinca was a young woman. Buddha's enemies bribed her to accuse Buddha of having lived with her. She put on a wooden globe and appeared like a pregnant woman. Month after month did Buddha's enemies revile him. Buddha remained silent and serene. In the ninth month, this wicked woman appeared at Buddha's evening *satsang*. In the presence of the people, she accused Buddha of having lived with her and asked him to provide her with a place for her approaching confinement. Buddha remained calm. In gentle words he said to her:—"Sister! whether thy words be true or not true, nobody knows but you and I." At these words, the woman's wooden globe fell down! The people saw she was not pregnant! They hooted her and pursued her; she confessed the truth and asked for pardon.

Devadatta was Buddha's cousin and disciple, but turned a traitor. Devadatta wished to be the Leader. He spread false reports against Buddha and, later, hired men to murder the Master. They went to kill; they remained to revere him! In his sacred presence they were converted. They fell at his feet; they confessed their sin; they asked for pardon; they repented and became his disciples.

Buddha's life of singular purity and singular love soon conquered all opposition. Buddha came to be revered as the "Teacher of men and the Gods." Princes deemed it a proud privillege to pay homage to him. He had the simplicity of a child and the humility of a saint. A prince invited Buddha and carpeted the mansion with fine gaudy sheets. Buddha would not walk on them. He kept standing at the entrance till they were taken up. Cobblers and barbers and other men of "inferior" castes were welcomed by him to his *satsang*. Buddha had profound reverence for the poor. Before he passed away, in 483 B.C., his message had travelled to millions.

Buddha's teaching is preserved for us, partly, in the books called "Tripitaka." The word means "Three Baskets." The Teaching was brought together in volumes, receptacles, "baskets" of palm-leaves. The title, "Tripitaka," therefore, is significant. It reminds us that the period in which Buddha taught belonged to a rural age, as the modern period belongs to a technological age.

In the age of Buddha, they came together to listen to the Master under the shade of trees,—far from the din and conflict of cities. They walked bare-footed through the fields, from village to village. It was a beautiful life they lived,—a two-fold life:—(1) a life of consecrated work in the fields and (2) a life of communion with Truth, at the feet of a holy one or in silence.

The "Three Baskets" are:—

(1) Of the "Three Baskets," the first is called "Vinaya." The word means "discipline." In "Vinaya," we are told of the *sadhanas*, the "disciplinary rules," which must be observed by those who would live spiritual lives.

(2) The second is named the "Sutta," i.e. "thread" or "threads." Buddha's words of wisdom, the Buddha-*bani*, Buddha's *upadeshes*, "discourses," interpreting the secret of true life.

(3) The third is named "Abhidhamma," i.e. *dhamma* showing forth the "foundations" of the teaching of Buddha.

The "Sayings" of Buddha are rich in thought, for they are radiant with the Light of the Spirit. Some of them I have put in free verse thus:—

[1]

May every living thing,
Weak or strong, tall or short,
Dwelling near or far away,
Born or yet in womb unborn,—
May everything on earth
Breathing out the breath of life,—
Be happy, full of bliss!

[2]

When, indeed, a man doth wrong to me,
I forget not this,—he foolishly doth go
Astray. And I feel that I must guard
Him still with love. The more of evil comes
From him to me, the more I feel
Must good go out of me to him!

[3]

O *bhikkhus*! know
That life is pain.
And pain arises out
Of dark desires.
And wisdom lies in this,—
The stilling of desire.
And so do all your work
As one detached:
Walk still the way of love!
Give help and sympathy
To the poor and lonely, to all
Who cry for comfort, healing help,
In this world of tears!

[4]

The bath of baths,—the holy bath,—
My brahmin-brother! is this indeed:—
Be kind to all,
And speak not false,
Nor kill thou life,
Nor take thou aught
Which is not thine!
In self-denial be thou strong!
Then, in truth, the water of any stream
Is Ganga or Gaya to thee!

[5]

Brethren!
If, indeed, the robbers cross you on the way,
And with a two-handed saw
Carve you in pieces, limb by limb,
And you harbour for them hatred in your hearts,
Know, then, you are not worthy of me,
Nor of the message I come to give!

[6]

The root is sorrow, know,—
Is *tanha*, is desire,—
The selfish thought that seeks
The pleasure of a part,
But not, alas! the Good of the Whole.
Know that desire, in its depths, is the sexual urge:
It stretches out the chain of life
Into pain that never ends!

[7]

Go ye into far-off lands
And preach to all the truth
That the poor and lowly,
The rich and the high,
Are all in verity one:
And that all the castes, too, mingle still
In this Religion of Compassion, Service, Truth,
As do the rivers in the sea!

"As a Lamp Into Darkness !"

From village to village, the Buddha moved with his message of the Noble Eightfold Path, until he came to the village of Nadika.

The beloved Ananda came and sat down beside him and Buddha taught the people, saying:—

> Rich is the fruit of contemplation,
> Adorned with right action:
> And rich is the fruit of the mind
> Adorned with contemplation.
> For, through contemplation the mind is freed
> From sensuality,
> From the false ego,
> From delusion and ignorance.

The Buddha moved on to Beluva, where the rainy season had set in. And the Master spake to Ananda thus:—

> Ananda!
> I, too, am now grown old;
> Full of years am I:
> My earth-journey is drawing to its close:
> I am turning eighty years of age:
> I have reached my sum of days.
> A worn-out cart.
> Can move only with care:
> So this body, Ananda!
> Can only move with care.
> Ananda! happy is my body
> When absorbed in devout meditation!

Then the Master passed on to the mango-grove of Chanda, the smith.

And there, the Blessed One had his meals in the dwelling-place of Chanda. And then there fell on him a sickness and sharp pains did come upon him. But he was self-possessed: he bore the pains, complaining not.

Then to Ananda the Master said:— "Let us go to Kusinara,"

"Even so, Lord!" said Ananda.

And they went.

And, on the way, the Blessed One grew weary and he rested beneath a tree and said:— "Ananda! fold the robe and spread it for me. For I am weary, Ananda! and I must rest awhile."

And the robe was spread. And the Blessed One asked for fresh water to drink.

And Ananda took Buddha's bowl and brought in it water from a stream.

And there came a brahmin. To him the Buddha spoke of calm in contemplation and of the mind which keeps clear of the vanities and shows of life.

And the Brahmin said:—

As a lamp into darkness
Are your words, O Buddha!
Accept me as a disciple.

The Buddha, in his eightieth year, lay down by the riverside, between two Sal trees, their blossoms dropping on his body. And he gave a message to Ananda, saying:—"Ananda! be ever intent on good!"

Ananda lovingly gazed on the Master, absorbed in his words. Ananda felt that the Lord was soon to go. And Ananda's eyes were touched with tears. And Ananda, not wishing that the Buddha might see his tears, went into a neighbouring monastery and stood leaning against the door. And Ananda wept.

Again and again, did Ananda reproach himself with the thought:— "The Master is about to go. How kind has he been! Yet alas! I am still so far from the goal. I have not yet attained."

And the Master asked:— "Where, O monks, is Ananda?"

And they said to him:—"Ananda is gone to the monastery."

Then he said to a monk:—"Brother! go and tell him thus:— 'O Brother Ananda! the Master calls you!'"

And Ananda,—Buddha's beloved,—returned. And looking at him, the Buddha said:—

Ananda! do not weep.
All things decay and dissolve.
Ananda! for a long time
Have you served me;
For a long time have you been,

Near, very near to me.
By acts of a love that varies not,—
A love that is beyond all measure,—
And not by acts only
Buy, also, by words
And by thoughts of love
Have you been so near to me.
Ananda! be earnest in effort
And attain the Perfect Life!

And Ananda knelt and he hid his face.

And after a while, the Blessed One opened his eyelids and looked for the last time upon Ananda and other disciples. Yes, for the last time the disciples heard the Master's words:—

Behold now, brethren!
I ask you all, forget not this:—
All things are subject to decay.
Work out your salvation with diligence!

And, with deep emotion, they knelt about him. And the Blessed One departed!

At the age of over eighty years, Buddha went into *parinirvana*. Between the two Sal trees he lay, as they scattered flowers on him in a grove at Kusinara, in the country of the Mallas.

And trembling and in deep silence all the *bhikkhus* knelt before the Body of the departed Master. And all the brethren veiled their faces.

Then some of the *bhikkhus* cried aloud:—

Too soon has the Blessed One departed!
Too soon has the Happy One left us!
Too soon has the world's Incomparable Light
vanished!

But the more advanced among the *bhikkhus* said:—

Transient are all earthly things!
Transient are all corporeal things!
Transient are all earthly forms!

But Ananda wept all the night and could not be comforted.

The Mallas learnt of the Master's departure. They came weeping and did honour to the Body with music and garlands and processions for a space of six days. On the seventh day, the Body was carried by eight of their chieftains to a shrine outside the city on the East.

The final ceremony of cremation awaited the arrival of Buddha's disciple, Kasyapa, who, with five hundred *bhikkhus*, was approaching Kusinara.

On reaching the shrine, Kasyapa saluted with reverence the Body of the Buddha, then passed thrice round the funeral pyre. His companions,—the five hundred *bhikkhus*,—did the same. Kasyapa and his companions bowed down to the Body in homage every time they went round the funeral-pyre.

Rich was Buddha in wisdom, richer still in the inspiration of his life. He was a genius of will. He was a genius, too, of intellect. For forty years and more, he, who was born a prince, wandered about with a begging-bowl in his hands, from village to village, with his great message to the poor and the rich, the peasant and the prince. At dawn he rose each day and he taught all men, thinking not of caste or clan or colour or creed. He taught rich merchants, no less than the untouchables, the Way of Deliverance. And he entered into the hearts of the people. He became the Beloved of Aryavarta.

Again and again, he spake to the *bhikkhus* thus:—

> Wander through the land
> With the message of healing
> And the message of light.
> And in the midst of darkness
> Kindle ye the light that heals!
> Thus go ye forth to places near and places far!
> And, filled with compassion,
> Bring happiness to multitudes,
> Bring new life to all!

And again:—

> This triple truth
> Teach ye to all:—

The generous heart,
The kindly speech,
The life of compassion and service,—
These be the things
That make Humanity new!

Junnuna Misri: A Pilgrim Of Eternity

[1]

AN INTERPRETER OF Christian thought spoke of Egypt as "the land of darkness." He spoke what history will reject as untrue. Egypt was, once, a centre of "schools of initiation," a home of "mysteries." Heraclitus and Pythagoras confessed that they had been initiated in Egypt into the "mysteries," and Neo-Platonism had its centre in Alexandria. In Egypt there were groups of young men who studied the Nile and the heavens: and in Egypt were developed architecture, engineering, astronomy and astrology, at which we moderns may well marvel.

Cairo was the richest city west of the Indus: Cairo was the homeland of medieval music in Islam: Cairo was a shrine of art and culture. In this land of a thousand lutes, we have, at this very hour, the oldest existing University,—the University of el-Azhar. It is an international University, drawing pupils from all the Muslim world,—from Persia to Zanzibar, from China and Japan. A remarkable University! Students pay no fees: teachers receive no pays. Today el-Azhar has some ten thousand students and three hundred professors. And it is an impressive sight to see groups of students in the cloisters of a mosque,—a thousand year old mosque,—each group squatting in a semicircle before a revered teacher. Impressive, too, is the great "Hall of Wisdom" in the University. In this great University, God is, to students and professors, a Reality, not an abstraction. Five times a day they bend themselves in reverence before God: their faith in a Higher Power has much to teach the "modern" man. And their reverence for the Prophet, Mahomed, is profound. Was he not a man of deep humility and prayer? He claimed no more than that he had a "message for mankind." "I am one like unto you,—a man," he said. And on the day he was leaving the world for his Unseen Home, he said to them:—"Do not rush at one another's throat after I go: for, one day, you will have to face Allah, Who will required you to answer for your sins."

And Egypt was, for some time, a spiritual teacher of Greece and Rome. Egypt became a homeland of friars and *fakirs*. In Egypt lived, in the Muslim era, when Khalifas ruled Baghdad, a great teacher of spiritual science, a "master" of wisdom. They called him "Misri (Egyptian),"—more fully, "Junnuna Misri." He rose to a vision of the Truth that is universal,—the Truth that discards neither Muslim nor Hindu, neither Christian nor Buddhist, neither Greek nor Jew, but embraces them all in a Unity that the sages of India have adored as the *Eka meva Dvityam*, "the One without a second." Pure pearls,—gems of the purest ray serene,—Have i found in the words of this "Egyptian Master." And I have marvelled at the man and his depth of perception and significance. Listen to what he says:—

* Common is the sight of men who bear misfortune: but how uncommon the sight of the blessed ones who bear the buffets of fate, yet do not lose the peace of the soul!

* If thou hast met God, He is enough—the one True Friend in life: If thou has not met Him, meet them who are His Friends: and thou wilt be happy.

* Thou cravest for company? Then be in the company of those who have risen above the distinctions of "I" and "Thou." Theirs are consecrated lives!

* Never think of any creature as mean: never think of anyone as inferior to thee: open the inner Eye that beholdeth the Counternance of God and thou wilt see that in all creatures shineth the One Glory!

* Meditation on God is my food: His praise is my drink: and to bear witness to His Glory is my garment.

On these and many other sayings of this Teacher have I meditated, from time to time,and have found them charged with the Wisdom of the Gita and the Teaching of the Upanishads. In the thought of this "Egyptian Master" I find a psychology which sees the vanity of logic and argumentation, an ethic which sees the God beyond all "gods,"—the "illusory" appearances of the "surface" we call the world,—and a philosophy which sees that deeper than science or politics or industry is the meditation which reveals the depth of life concealed from those who live as captives in the heavy chains of "desire."

[2]

God works in strange ways His wonders to perform. In a strange way is Junnuna's life transformed. The transformation is nothing short of a revolution. He is young: he hears, again and again, of a holy man, Junnuna goes to meet this man of God,—this *tapasvin* (ascetic). Junnuna finds that the *tapasvin* is suspended in a tree, his head downwards, his feet upwards, and he is repeatedly saying to himself:—"O thou, my body! if thou wilt not co-operate with me in my spiritual aspirations and discipline, I shall torture thee thus! I shall keep thee hungry and thirsty until thou diest!"

Junnuna weeps as he hears these words. The *tapasvin* hears the sobs of Junnuna and, calling him, says:—"Look! who is there who will have compassion upon one who is not only full of sins but is not ashamed of sins?"

Junnuna asks:—"I understand you not. Tell me clearly what you mean."

The *tapasvi* says:—"Look? this body of mine refuses to help me in the service and worship of the Lord. This body would rather mix with the crowds and make merry. So I am teaching it the practice of abstinence."

Junnuna asks:—Have you committed murder or some other heinous sins?"

Tapasvi:—"No!"

Junnuna:—"Are you a great *vairagi* (ascetic)?"

Tapasvi:—"No! No! If you would see a great *vairagi*, ascend this mountain and see him on the top!"

* * *

Junnuna goes up the mountain and sees that at the door of a cottage is sitting a *tapasvi* (ascetic): his one foot is inside the cottage: the other foot, which is cut, is outside the cottage; ants have surrounded the foot. Junnuna draws near, salutes him, and asks what the matter is.

The *tapasvi* says:—"I sat in my cottage one day, and I saw in front of me a young woman coming out of her house. I saw her and was bewitched with her beauty. I longed to see her lovely face again. So I stood up and I had hardly put one foot outside my cottage, when I heard suddenly a voice saying to me:—'O ascetic! art thou not ashamed of thyself? Thou hast glorified the Lord for thirty years: thou dost call thyself a *bhakta* (devotee of the Lord): yet art thou entangled in the snare of Satan! Beware! Rise above the glamour of that young woman! Awake! Awake! Or be thou fallen in the pit of hell!'

"And listening to these words, I trembled. I cut the foot which I had placed outside the cottage. I threw the foot outside: since then I have sat there, patiently awaiting what is to come. Brother! why hast thou come to me, a sinner? If thou wouldst see a true *Mahatma* (saint), then go forward: thou wilt see him on yon mountainheight!"

Junnuna is unable to ascent so high. So he returns to the *tapasvi* and enquires of him all about the *Mahatma*. The *tapasvi* says:—"On yon mountain-heights sits a true *sadhu*, a *Mahatma*. One day, there came to him a man who said:—'If a man will not earn, how will he live? Life depends on your daily exertions: What can the grace of God do,—unaided by human efforts?' Hearing this, the *Mahatma* said to himself:—'Is not the grace of God all-sufficient? If a man will not work hard, does God become impotent to help him? I resolve not to eat what a man may bring to me.' And for several days the *tapasvi* ate nothing. Then God guarded the man's life: how? The bees came and built a home there: and the honey of that home was eaten by the *tapasvi*: his life was saved."

Junnuna hears and his heart is filled with faith in God and God's unfailing love. "He will take care of me," say Junnuna; "He will not leave me in the dust."

* * *

Junnuna returns home: and on the way he sees a blind bird alighting from a tree: and Junnuna says to himself:—"Whence does this blind bird get his daily food?" What does Junnuna see? The blind bird scratches the earth and underneath are a few grains and drops of water: the bird eats and drinks and is perched again upon the tree. Junnuna's faith in God is intensified. Junnuna's life is revolutionised: he becomes new!

Not yet is he become a "Master": but he has received his first lesson. He now longs to live a New life: he longs to be desireless: he begins to see the world of life in the light of God,—the Providence of all! he sees that in him starts the process of a new creative life. New aspiration takes its birth within him: he begins to see the vanity of earthly ambitions, of honours and fame: he grows in the strength to renounce!

[3]

But he is not yet pure enough. "God, the great Master," he says, "will purify me and in His good time make me a child of His Light,—a child of Grace,—and, passing through the Fire, I, too, may shine as gold thrice-refined!"

Junnuna prays intensely:—"O Lord! make me Thine. Let not the world overwhelm me! But fill me with Thy Presence that I may see Thy Beauty everywhere!"

One day, he goes to a river to have his bath and offer his prayers to God, Junnuna enters into the river, when lo! and behold! his eyes and turned to the roof of a radiant house. One is standing on the roof and Junnuna's eyes are there-transfixed! He is absorbed in a form of wondrous beauty. A young woman is standing on the roof, and Junnuna looks on! Junnuna has lost himself in this vision of loveliness. And, waking from this vision, he says to her:—"O beautiful one! are you married? And what is your name?"

And she answers:—"Junnuna! you are no stranger to me. Your name has travelled to me, and I was told that you were a *fakir*, a man of realisation, wisdom-filled, God-intoxicated. And when I saw you at a distance, I was filled with a longing to see you and be blessed. Now I see you near and now I know, alas! that earthly beauty bereaves you of reason and self-control!"

And longing to hear her more,—for to him her words were sweeter than honey,—he says:—"Speak to me more clearly, for my mind is confused. And true it is I feel, at this moment, like a drunken man!"

And she, in whose heart is love of God and love of the Saints of God, speaketh,—her eyes radiant with compassion and humility:—"Junnuna! if you were a *fakir*, you would not be distracted by a form: if you were a man of realisation, you would know that what endureth not is, for ever and ever, only a dream: if you were wisdom-filled, your heart would rise above desire and be lifted to the beatific vision of eternal Truth: if you were God-intoxicated, your joy would be in Him, not in a frail, fickle creature of dust and desire,—in Him, and His Light which is brighter than the sun, the moon and the stars!"

So saying, she vanishes. And Junnuna turns this way and that. She hath vanished: and tears tremble in his eyes: and for some moments he meditates upon her words and says to himself:—"What she hath said of me is true: every word of that radiant one had a ring of sincerity. It is true I am not yet become a true *fakir*; wisdom is still afar! For I see that in my heart is a flame, not a spring of the holy water that heals: and in mine eyes is still earthly desire, not the intoxication of the Eternal Name. What right have I to live? Death! O Death! Come and enfold me!"

[4]

Junnuna now enters into the waters of the Nile. He wishes to drown himself. The Nile is like the Indus,—a river rapid but erratic.

A merchant's boat is moving on the waters. Some one in the boat sees Junnuna being drowned and raises the cry:—"Save! O save!" The boat stops and picks up Junnuna. He is saved, and he is beaten,—blow after blow falling upon his back and his face. The merchant strikes him, beats him black and blue. Why? The merchant has lost precious pearls and suspects Junnuna to be the thief! But Junnuna bears all the blows with the patience of a true *bhakta*. Junnuna says to himself:—"O Lord! Thou knowest all!" The lost pearls are, later, found elsewhere, and the merchant, on bended knee, tells Junnuna:—"Forgive me! I have beaten you and I have sinned!"

Junnuna never forgets what has happened,—never forgets the mercy of the Lord. "Yea, though I walk through the valley of the shadow of death, I will fear no evil: for Thou art with me. Thy rod and Thy staff,—they shall comfort me." The Lord hath saved Junnuna: the Lord hath punished him! He feels purified and he sheds tears in longing for the Lord. And he is out, again, in quest!

[5]

One day, as he goes up a mountain, he sees a number of men and women: they all are sick and afflicted: they have congregated in one place.

Junnuna asks:—"Why are so many come together in this place on mountain-heights? And they all are sick and afflicted!"

One of them says:—"In yon cottage dwells a *tapasvi*, a holy man: once a year he cometh out of his cottage and, with his healing breath, he heals the sick, and then enters again the cottage. Today is the annual day of pilgrimage to him: and so the crowds are come together here to see him and be healed."

After some time this holy man cometh out of his cottage. His body is so frail,—bones without flesh and blood: pallor is on his lips: his eyes are sunk in their sockets: but his face is radiant with a strange, un-earthly light. And as he comes out, he gazes with compassionate eyes on the men and women who are come to see him and be cured: then he lifts his eyes in supplication to the Heavens above: then he calls each patient to himself, and into each he breathes the breath of his benediction: he heals them, then goes back to his cottage. And as he goes, Junnuna clings to his feet and says:—"O holy one! thou hast cured so many: look thou on me, too, with eyes of compassion: for I, too, suffer. In the Name of Allah (God), I ask thee to heal me!"

And the Healer hears Junnuna and says:—"Junnuna! leave me! I am nothing. On the high Throne sitteth He, Who seeth all,—My Beloved, your Friend! Go to Him! Take shelter at His Feet! He will heal thee!"

And the holy man re-enters his cottage! And Junnuna learns to enter in the cave of his heart: and there he seeks the Lord until He finds him. For ever the Lord seeketh His own: He finds us first: then are we God-possessed, absorbed in the Eternal.

[6]

Junnuna now attracts some,—seekers of God. They come from towns and villages: they sit at his feet to learn of him the truths of spiritual life. They take his name afar: and in Egypt and Arabia and Turkestan they call him the "Egyptian Master." But they are not many. What a mercy of God when a great Teacher appears! Democracy makes a mistake in supposing that a crowd can understand and choose. Crowds lack comprehension. A "Master" is understood only by "prepared souls." And many do not understand the "Master:" they call him a "*kafir*": the *mullahs* (Muslim priests) hate him as a "heretic."

They carry reports to the Khalif of Baghdad. Egypt was, in those days, a province of this Khalif: and he is poisoned against the "Master." Junnuna is seized and brought to Baghdad. In silence stands he before the Khalif. So Jesus stood before Pilate. Junnuna speaks not a word, but his eyes are aglow with a great Light. His silence is eloquent. An old man draws nigh to him and whispers to him:—"Your eyes and your silence bear witness to your wisdom: you are not a culprit: you are a servant of God, a messenger of His Truth: and without His Will no one can touch a hair of your head. Mind not the *mullahs*: if it be God's Will that you go to prison, in prison, we know, you will glorify Him!"

And Junnuna is sent to jail! Again and again, have the messengers of God been imprisoned, persecuted, crucified, shot to death. But Truth is not stifled. Truth shines radiant on the gallows and in jail.

Junnuna goes to jail with a smile on his lips! The sun is still upon the hill-tops: a few of the Master's disciples are with him at the jail-gate: their tears are flowing fast. "Weep not," he says to them; "I wish to go in peace. And nought happens without the Will of Allah: in Him is our peace!"

One of the wisest, the purest and the best of men goes into jail,—unmourned except by a few. The majority are under the influence of the *mullahs*: they call him an "atheist"! And this "atheist" taught that there is but one God in Allah, the Eternal, is the peace of man! The majority fail to understand the "Master": men in crowds are swayed by harangues, not thought. Plato urges that numbers are no index to wisdom and that crowds are ruled by demagogues, "who go ringing on in long harangues, like brazen pots which when struck, continue to sound till a hand is put upon them!" A society is in peril when led by its demagogues, not is purest and wisest men.

Junnuna is in jail for forty days. Hunger enfeebles him: but he is steadfast in fast and prayer. On being released he walks, but he is so weak that he falls, again and again, on the ground: his head bleeds. In this state he is brought before the Khalifa. The news spreads quickly abroad: his disciples gather in the garden of the Khalifa's mansion: the disciples see the Master again but are filled with indignation when they see him tired, exhausted, worn out, with blood-marks on his head!

Junnuna stands before the Khalifa in the garden: and the courtiers are around the Khalifa. He looks at Junnuna and is moved by what he sees,—a Teacher dear to his disciples as the Master, in tattered clothes, blood-stained, yet with eyes glowing with a strange, mystic light. The Khalifa offers Junnuna a seat and asks him to sit down. Then follows a little talk between the two.

Khalifa:—Junnuna! you are now free. But see that you teach nothing subversive of the state or the social order.

Junnuna:—I teach as I have been taught.

Khalifa:—What have you been taught?

Junnuna:—This, O ruler of men! that if a society would have life, it must live by the law of love, and that if a state would be strong it must be ruled by guardians of the moral law and they must live a simple frugal life,—as lived the early Khalifas. They lived a hard and simple life: they eschewed luxury: they revealed Allah, the Eternal, in daily life: their aspiration was not long prayers but communion with the Divine in silence and alms to the poor: they were the friends and guardians of the people: they were the sons of Light!

As Junnuna speaks, the Khalifa listen and quietly drinks in the words, one by one: and as Junnuna closes his little but lyrical talk, the Khalifa bursts into tears. And the courtiers and disciples, too, weep. There is, for a few minutes, a hush of holy silence. Then the Khalifa falls at Junnuna's feet and says:—"Master! forgive me.

...s thy disciple."

... has happened! Such "miracles" have happened, ...gain, in the history of the God-men, the mystics of Illumination, the sons of Light! The Khalifa now requests the "Master" to stay in the palace: the Khalifa serves the "Master" with wonderful devotion. Junnuna has no thought of founding a sect: his gentle life influences many and his teaching regarding Allah, the Eternal, travels to towns and villages: he teaches that Allah, the Eternal, is the Light of the dawn and the setting sun, is the Beauty of the blue sky and the Breath of the living air, is the Wisdom of the pure in heart and the Radiance of the life of His lovers and saints.

For some time he stays in the palace, then takes leave of the Khalifa and returns to Egypt.

[7]

Back to his homeland,—at last! Junnuna is out of his seclusion to give his message to multitudes. He thrills them: they call him Junnuna Misri: they revere him as a "Master" of wisdom: and crowds are moved by his "Sayings." Here are a few:—

* When the Lord showers His love upon His servants, He becomes their Eyes, their Ears, their Hands. Then through Him they see, they hear, they speak, they give and take!
* Listen not to them who praise thee for gifts or charity or good deeds. The praise is not thine: the praise is His who giveth all!
* First be a servant of God: and until thou art become His servant, do not say thou art Divine: else wouldst thou go into the deepest darkness of Hell!
* Two marks there be of him what is a true lover of the Lord:—(1) he is stable in censure and praise; and (2) he does his duty without a desire for fruit.
* Be not attached to them who are to the world attached: do not flatter them who give money or gifts: and hate no man who causeth thee harm!

Many find a solace in these wonderful words. Are they not full of assurance, illumination and inspiration?

[8]

Junnuna spends the eve of his life in Egypt. The Egyptian Master's name travels far and wide. His influence grows: his life fascinates many: they meditate on the grandeur of his sufferings and the glory of his teaching. The *mullahs* continue to call him an "infidel," an "atheist": but he has lighted a fire which not all their efforts can quench. Fate has written that Junnuna should belong to all: from province to province spreads the message of this man who has searched and found, has wandered and suffered and, at last,—attained! In his heart there is room for all,—the Sunni and the Shiah, the Jew and the Christian, the Greek and the Gentile. And to all men in his quiet, gentle way, he points the Way of Blessedness.

Junnuna is become a servant of Allah: and He hath looked upon His servant with love: and out of the mouth of Junnuna speaketh Allah and out of the eyes of His servant looketh the Lord.

"What is your food?" -they ask Junnuna. and he answers:- "Communion with God is the daily food of my life!"

"Why are you so patient with your opponents?"- -they ask him. And he answers:-"Truth is the Sword of God, and it never fails!"

"Who is the true giver of alms?"-he is asked. And in answer he says :- "The true giver is he who never opens his ears to hear his praise. The true giver understands that all praise is the Lord's and that unto Him is all glory!"

"Is not man divine?"-they ask him. and he says:- "Yes; but the proof that a man is divine is this, that he is ever-increasingly a servant of Allah,the Eternal!'

"And what are the signs of a true servant?"

Junnuna says: -"Two signs. (1) He suffers; and (2) in the midst of all sufferings he keeps his mind unruffled: he lives in the presence of Great Peace."

Three of the rules of spiritual life he gives to his disciples impress me much. These are:-(1) keep away from men addicted to this world; (2) never flatter the rich nor those who give in charity; and (3) never hate those who harm you.

"What is the secret of the dedicated life" -he is asked. and he says:-"The secret lies in self-forgetfulness:forget yourself, forget your work, and see that your hope is in God alone,-in none else, in none else!"

And this, too, he says:-"The world is whatever keeps you away from God! And he is a low-caste man who walketh not the way that leadeth unto the Lord!"

A disciple asks him:-"Master! whose company may I keep?" And the Master says:-"His who has no sense of 'thine and 'mine!"

In a discourse, the Master says:-"Regard not the creatures as mean or inferior to you. Open the Inward Eye and you will behold the glory of Allah, the Eternal,-in all"

speaking to a man who has spent years in sin, he says:-"Let not your past sit as a burden upon you! Think of the Present and the God of the Present. In Him be absorbed and sing His Name!"

"Who is the happy man?" asks a disciple. And the Master says:-"He who knows God and is in Him absorbed!"

Speaking of the "Steps of Ascent," the Master says:-"He who would ascend to Allah, the Eternal, must mount up the following steps:- (1) giving up running after the things of the world; (2) aversion for worldly pleasure; (3) purity; and (4) each day growing in the love of God!"

In these "Sayings" of the Master is a treasure of infinite value which will never perish. Surely, these are not the "Sayings" of an "impious atheist" but of a singular man, God-absorbed and dedicated to the life Divine!

[9]

One day, he is crossing a field: he finds it covered with snow. A man is near: he is throwing grains on the ground. The Master asks:-"Brother! the ground is covered with snow: why do you throw the grains on the ground?" The man answers:-"Yes; today the ground is vovered with snow, and the birds know not where to go for food. For them I throw these grains on the ground that the birds may eat them when they can. The Lord will accept these little grains which I offer in devotion to the little birds."

Soon after, the Master goes to Mecca and he sees the very man there as a "devotee" of God going round the Kaaba. Seeing Junnuna, this man says:-"How are you? You see how Allah has accepted my humble, little service to the birds! I threw the grains on the ground; see the 'fruit' now! God has had mercy on me and brought me to this holy place." "Yes," says Junnuna, "the Lord accepts every little grain offered to His creatures with devotion!"

So Sri Krishna says to Arjuna in the Gita:- "A leaf, a flower, a fruit, a little water: I accept every little gift offered with devotion."

[10]

Beautiful was the Master's life! Beautiful, too, was his death! Serene he lies on his death-bed.

A desciple asks him:-"Master! tell us what is your desire at this moment?"

The Master says:-"This only, that He be near me as I am nearing death, so that He,-my Friend,-may enter again into my song and reveal again His radiant Face to me!"

So saying, the Master sings a song in Arabic,-a song filled with singular love and longing for Allah, the Eternal.

Then comes his last utterance before he passes on to his Abode:-"I am absorbed in the grace and love of my Beloved,-of Allah, the Eternal."

junnuna lived God-absorbed. And God-absorbed, his soul ascended to the Home of Glory. The sun shone in splendour at that time: and, as in the case of St. Francis.—a lover of God and of God's creatures,-so in the case of Junnuna,—a lover of God and the little birds of God,—group after group of birds came and fluttered over him and received his blessings in the hour of his death.

* * *

His thoughts wre deeper than the sea: and in his life was a beauty brighter than the beauty of the moon and the stars. In the years to be, pilgrims from India to Egypt will come to the spot, where Junnuna breathed the last benediction of his earth-life, and bow in lowly reverence to his blessed name and say:—"Here was one, who taught that wisdom, not wealth, is the Way,—one, who saw the Face of God unveiled, as did Kasyapa and Agastya, Yagnavalkya and Brihasptai and other holy Rishis of India, in the long, long ago!"

Rabia: A Saint Of The Silent Way

[1]

SITTING, ONE EVENING, in solitude, I read the following words:—

I have made Thee the Companion of my heart.
The groaning and the yearning of the lover of God
will continue until the heart has found
Its rest in the Beloved.
The Beloved of my heart is the Guest of my soul.
My peace is in solitude: but my Beloved is ever
with me.
Nothing can take the place of His Love:
It is the test for me among mortal beings.
O Healer of souls !
The heart feeds upon its aspiration:
I aspire towards Union with Thee:
And this aspiration heals my soul.
My hope is for union with Thee.
This Union is the goal of my quest !

The words filled my heart. "The Beloved of my heart is the Guest of my soud!"I repeated these words, again and again. I remembered they were the words of a great Muslim mystic, Rabia: I have not forgotten them. Rabia remains enshrined in my heart. I regard her as one of the greatest mystics of Islam.

I often call her the "Mira of Islam." Mira was a queen: Rabia was a poor orphan. But Mira renounced her palace and all her possessions and became poor in the service of God. Both Mira and Rabia sang songs rich in *bhakti* (devotion). Both were mystics: a mystic is in tune with the Infinite. Both Mira and Rabia were God-intoxicated. Attar, a name linked with the great Sufi mystics like Ghazali, Rumi and Hafiz, speaks of Rabia in the following words:—

Veiled was she with the veil of purity:

On fire was she with love and longing for God:
Filled was she with the aspiration to be consumed
in His glory:
Lost was she in union with the Divine:
Set apart was Rabia in the seclusion of holiness:
Accepted was she by men as a second spotless
Mary !

[2]

Born at Basra about 717 A.D. Rabia died in A.D. 801. She was born of humble parents. She was a little girl when her mother died. Rabia was the fourth sister in the family. All members of the family were scattered by a famine. Rabia was kidnapped and sold as slave for six *dirhams* (silver coins). Her master gave her hard work to do. Alas! he beat her, again and again. Rabia complained not: patience is a mark of a true sufi. Rabia fasted in the day to find time to cope with her work. She slept a few hours only.

Her master continued to be cruel to her. One day, she ran away. She had not proceeded far when she got a fall and broke her left hand. In deep agony she cried to God:-

O Lord !
My gracious Lord !
Thou knowest
I have no father:
I have no mother:
I am an orphan:
As a prisoner
I spend my time
Day and night, in suffering and pain:
And now my left hand, too, is broken !
Is it that Thou, my divine Master,
Art not pleased with me ?
Tell me, Lord !
Why art Thou angry with me ?

In this hour of her agony, a Voice spoke to her from within:—

My child !
Cast all thy care on Him
Who speaketh to thee,-thy Lord !
Soon will thy suffering be over,
But thy witness will stand
Before the pure ones of the Earth !

She returned to her master's house.

One night, her master happened to look down through a window of the house and saw Rabia in prayers.

He listened: he heard her praying thus:-

O Lord !
Thou knowest,—
Thou knowest all !
Thou knowest the aspirations of my heart !
Thou knowest I long to obey Thee !
Thou knowest the light of my eyes
Is in the service of Thy Holy Feet !
If, indeed, the matter rested with me,
I should not cease even for an hour to serve Thee.
But it is Thy Will that I be a slave to a creature,
And much of my time is spent in his service !

The master heard Rabia's touching words and was moved. He looked up: he saw that above her head was shining a lamp suspended without a chain. He saw her enveloped in Light. He saw, too, that the whole house was illuminated by a mysterious Light.

The master was deeply impressed: he was afraid, too,at the sight. He said to himself:-"Grievously have I sinned. I have made a saint of Allah a slave in my house!"

He realised that Rabia was one of God's elect. He repented. And early in the morn, he went to her and said:- "O thou, whom God hath blessed! I knew thee not. God in His mercy opened my eyes last night. I saw thee at prayer. I will not let thee serve me any longer. Stay in my house and be happy. Let *me* serve thee!"

Rabia said:- "My master! you have given me food for so many days. I feel grateful, I now ask of thee one thing only,-freedom. Be merciful to me and let me go where I will, and serve my God in freedom."

[3]

There are three types of men (and women):-

1. There are men of the world: their life is centred in the little "self." They are indifferent to the realities of Religion.

2. There are men who build life in 'reason." They argue, they think of God in terms of His "attributes" and His "manifestations" in Nature. These men are intellectual, logical. They, too, render service to the cause of Religion.

3. There are men of the "mystical" temperament. They are children of the Spirit. They perceive God intuitively. Their goal is ecstatic union with the Life Divine.

Rabia belonged to the third type.

She believed in meditation and prayer. Her prayer was not merely a fixed formula,-an obligatory prayer at an appointed hour. Rabia's prayer was unceasing, silent intercourse with God. This prayer is, in Islam, called *dhikr*, i.e. continuous repetition of the Name of God. In Vaishnava literature, this "prayer" is named "*Hari-Nama*":the true Vaishnava repeats it in his *kirtan*, again and again. How often did not Haridas repeat the Divine Name everyday before he ate his meals! Sri Chaitanya and his devoted followers purified the atmosphere of Nadia and, later, of Jagannath Puri by repeated utterance of the Divine Name:-"*Hari bol!*" "*Hari bol!*" (sing the Name of the Lord!")

And Rabia practised *tawakul*,-trust in the Lord. Your "intellectual" man reasons and says: "Money must be earned in order that the needs of life may be fulfilled." The child of the Spirit "works," yet believes that God is the great Giver. The mystic looks up to Him in daily life and, even when ill, believes that medical aid itself will not do good unless blessed by the Divine Spirit. Rabia was poor: she accepted poverty as God's gift to her. Her friends offered her material help, again and again. She said, again and again, that there was One who looded after her, helped her and healed her. She said:—

> Verily, I ask not for worldly things from Him to whom the world belongs. I ask not: for I know he does for me what is always for my good.
>
> How then should I ask for worldly things from men to whom the world does not belong?

"The best thing for the servant who desires to be near the Lord," said Rabia, "is to posess nothing in this world or in the next,- nothing save the Lord." she coveted no Paradise. Not in fear of Hell, not in desire of Heaven, but in pure aspiration to commune with God was the secret she taught, of true worship.

One of her friends went into her house in her old age and found there only four things:-(1) a mat; (2) a screen; (3) an earthen-ware jug for water; and (4) a bed which served, also, as her prayer-carpet.

She believed in "renunciation" as a law of spiritual life. Remarkable was her asceticism. When one of her acquaintances suggested that he would ask some of his kinsmen to get her a servant who would do the work of her house,-sweep the floor, cleanse the utensils, fill the water-jug for her,-she said:- "The whole world belongs to my Divine Master: and He will do for me what He knows is the best for me." "Trust in God," she said. "What He does for you is the best for you!

"One day, a friend (Hasan of Basra) came to visit her. He saw a wealthy merchant of Basra at the door of Rabia's cell with a purse of gold: the merchant stood at the door, weeping.

"Why do you weep?" asked Hasan.

The merchant said:- "Rabia is the great ascetic of this age: if she were not in our midst, we would perish. Her blessings sustain us and keep us alive. Alas! she lives in extreme poverty. I have brought for her a little gold! My fear is, she may tell me, 'Take it back: I want nothing!' If you will be so good as to plead for me, she may be pleased to accept my offer."

Hasan gave the message to RAbia. She looked at him and said:-

> God provids for those who revile Him: will He not provide for those who love Him?

He sustains those who speak unworthily of Him: will He not sustain me whose soul overflows with love for Him?

Ever since I have known Him, I have turned away from men to Him who is the Giver of all!

Rabia loved to regard herself as a "servant of the Lord". And "the servant who desires to be near to his Lord'. she said, "should possess nothing in this world or the next save the Lord alone!"

[4]

Repentance, *tawakul*, prayer and love-I regard as the four-fold treasure of Rabia.

Rabia often said that repentance (*tawba*) was the very first step on the Spiritual Way. It is the first "station" in the Way to the Perfect Life. And repentance, she taught, was a gift from God. On one occasion, she said;- "How can anyone repent unless the Lord gives him repentance and accepts him?" "Seeking forgiveness merely with the tongue," she said, "is the sin of lying!"After repentance comes "conversion" (*inabat*). Then comes renunciation(*zuhd*).

Then comes trust in God (*tawakul*). Rabia was poor:poverty did not frighten her. She surrendered her life to God. She feared not, for she had *tawakul*: "God will provide!"

Prayer, said Rabia, was free and intimate intercourse with God. Prayer was more than the prescribed *nimaz*, and other religious observances. In her life she bore witness to the truth that prayer was communion with God. Every spot was, to her, sacred as a mosque, and everyday the word arose in her heart:-"My Beloved!"Prayer was heart-to-heart converse with God. Prayer was spontaneous outpouring of the heart to God. Here is one of her prayers on which I have meditated, again and again:-

O my Lord!

If, indeed, Thou hast bestowed on me a share of this world, I pray to Thee to bestow it on those who deny Thee or revile Thy Name.

And if, indeed, Thou hast decreed that I should have a share of the next world, I pray this humble prayer:-"Give not the share to me, but give it to those who glorify Thee and Thy Name!"

For Thou, O Lord art enough for me. I need nothing else, nothing else!

Love or ecstatic vision of the Beloved,-was the goal of Rabia's life. The highest aspiration of Rabia's heart is expressed in the following verses:-

Two ways I love Thee:-
My "selfish love," love of my "happiness":
And next, "perfect love", the love which, indeed, is worthy of Thee.
Tis selfish love that I do nought
Save think on Thee excluding all beside:
But the perfect love, the purest love,
Which is Thy Love,
Shines forth when the veils which hide Thee fall
And I do gaze on Thee !

Yes,-the "perfect love," the "purest love," is "illumination": in it the "veil" is raised and the worshipper, the bhakta, the devotee sees the Beloved, face to face. In the "purest love" you see the Divine Beauty and you experience "mystical union" with God. This "mystical union" is referred to in a tradition of the Prophet:-

God said:- "My servant draws nigh unto Me and I love him. And when I love him, I am his ear, so that he hears by Me,-and his eye, so that he sees by Me,-and his tongue, so that he speaks by Me,-and his hand, so that he takes by Me!"

In this love, the "mystical love", the motive is not *fear* of God and of the "wrath to come" but "ecstatic communion" with the Divine.

You start then with repentance, which comes to him on whom is the grace of God. You proceed to spiritual disciplines of which an important one is renunciation or poverty. The basis of poverty is *tawakul*, ie. dependence on God. You grow in "prayer" which deepens into *dhikr*, constant repetition of the Name of Allah. So are you purified and gradually you rise to illumination, to gnosis (ma'rifa), which is "knowledge" and, at last, you attain to "communion with

God" which is reflected in the lives of saints who behold the Beloved with purified hearts. When love of the heart communes with the Beloved you reach the goal: and loving God, you grow in the love of your fellow-beings and, indeed, of all His creatures.

In the consummation of love, there is the annihilation of "I," "ego," the lower self. Your life, then, becomes a mirror of God. "You" are no more: the "I" has vanished! The aspiration, then, of the *salik*, the "traveller" on the Path is:-

Betwixt me and Thee
There lingers yet an "it is I !"
That torments me !
Ah ! of Thy grace, take away
This "I" from between us !

Rabia went through spiritual disciplines in order to achieve "mystical union" with God. Of this sings the great Sufi poet of Iran:-

Happy the moment
When we are seated
In the palace,-Thou and I !
With two forms
And with two figures
But with one soul,-Thou and I !

Pure and profound was Rabia's love for God. He was her Beloved. Her hand was sought in marriage by a number of men: she declined all offers. She said:-

Marriage ! How is it possible for me ?
I have ceased to exist:
I am no longer "I" !
I exist in him:
I am altogether His !
I live in the shadow of His command !
Not from me,
But from Him
Must a man ask for me
In marriage !

Rabia lived in the presence of the Purest One; to Him she gave herself, her heart and its purest love. And is it not true that if a man surrenders himself to Him, He,-the Lord,-surrenders Himself to him? Blessed, thrice- blessed was Rabia. Bayazid, the Sufi, rightly said:-"whoever seeth a God-man is blessed: he hath conquered all ills!"

[5]

Rabia was among the earliest exponents of the Sufi Way of life and the Sufi view of Love Divine. In the Sufi Way there are three journeys:-

1. The first is "Journey to God" (*sayar ila'llah*). In this journey the *salik*, the pilgrim, the aspirant,-the jignasu, to use a term of Hindu thought,-travels from the "world of creation" to the "world of Reality", often called *Haqiqat-i-Muhammadi.*

2. The second is "Journey in God" (*sayar fi'llah*). In this the *salik*, the aspirant is absorbed into the Divine Essence. Arriving at this stage, the Hindu seer exclaimed:-"*Tat twamasi*!" "That art thou!" That,-the Divine Essence,-is thy Goal! That,-is the one Reality wherein thou art to abide as thy Home! Well exclaimed the Muslim mystic:-

I am in Him whom I love !
We are two spirits in one Body !
In me, see thou Him !
And seeing Him, well mayst thou see us both !

3. The third is "journey from God" (*sayar ani'llah*). This is the journey back to the world of "manifestation." In the second journey, you enter into fana, annihilation. In the third journey, you enter into *baqa*, subsistence. You are on the plane of manifestation, yet are established in the Eternal.

Rabia was among the first singers and interpreters of the Doctrine of the Heart. "All that eyes behold," said a Muslim mystic, "belongs to earthly knowledge, but what the Heart beholds belongs to Certainty," therefore, to Eternity. "If you would be a true seeker," Rabia said, "go within and purify yourself, renouncing the inward sins." Going within, you will behold the Light! "Verily, knowledge is Light," said Abu Talib "which God breathes out in the Heart!"

Rabia, too, taught the Doctrine of God's Grace: it protects the seeker, and the greatest protection is his who learns to obey Him in all situations, In obeying the Will Divine is the true wisdom of life!

[6]

Like Mira, Rabia cried, again and again:-"I can no longer live without Thee, Beloved! And when she died to "selfhood," she rejoiced and cried:-"Blessed am I:I am Thine, Beloved!"

Rabia, I call the Mira of Islam, Christian writers have called her the "Moslem St. Teresa." Alike Mira, Teresa and Rabia had a perception of the goal of the mystic- a perception of that Kingdom which is our "Home,"-this earth-life being the journey of"pilgrims" to our true Homeland. Rabia refers to it in beautiful terms:-

Beloved !
My aspiration is but one;-
To remember Thee and Thee alone
Above all the things of the Earth !
This, also, is the longing in my heart,
That in the next world, too,
I may meet Thee alone, face to face !

Love with Rabia was dedication,-a total dedication of the will to the Will divine, of the heart to her Source. Rightly says a mystical writer of the West:-"It is the heart and never the reason which leads to the Absolute." The dedication of love, Rabia said, was detachment, was estrangement from all worldly affection. Again and again. breathes forth in Rabia's words the cry of love:-

Beloved ! Beloved !
I am all Thine !
Art Thou not all mine ?

Rabia had but one thought,-to spend her entire life for the Beloved. Like Mira, Rabia regarded hersefl as a moth"burnt with the touch of the Beloved's Face." "O heart," cried a great mystic of Iran, "hasten thither! For God will shine upon you and the world will seem to you a sweet garden instead of a terror."

Rabia, like the early Franciscans, practised complete renunciation of worldly things, of fame and wealth. Rabia's poverty was an expression of her detachment from the not-God and her devotion to the one God. Attachments become centres of conflicting interests: detachment saves you from complicated life and leads you on the right path,-the path of simplification. It is a great adventure this,-to strip yourself of everything and rely on the only One,-the Beloved!

Rabia sought God with the purest love of her heart: she sought Him not for anything"extern"but only for His sake. She asked for nothing in this world, nothing in the next. Over and over again, she ejaculated:-"Beloved! Thou art my all!" Her lover for Him was not a superficial emotion but a dedication, a total dedication of her will and her life-force to Him and His service. Rabia's love was not an "emotion" but a movement, a life-movement of her total self. In a beautiful tract by a mystic who has, like the Teachers of the Upanishads,withheld his name, we read the following significant words:-

Silence is not God !
And speaking is not God !
Fasting is not God !
And eating is not God !
Seclusion is not God !
Company is not God !
Nor may He be found
By any work of thy soul !
He may be found alone
By love of thine heart !
Not by reason
May He be known:
And He may not be gotten
By thought,
Nor concluded by understanding !
But He may be loved and chosen
With the true lovely will
Of thine heart !

Rabia's heart was filled with longing for the Beloved. Her life had but one aspiration to serve Him and be spent in His service. Such a love is fulfilled only in the annihilation of the "ego" or "self." Rabia's joy was only in this,-that her heart might be hidden in the Heart of the Beloved.

[7]

Rabia is rightly regarded as one of the earliest, Sufis. Her heart was *detached* from the world: passions were uprooted from her soul: desires were extirpated. Sannai has well observed:-"Ne'er can the world and Love together go!" Rabia realised that Allah's richest revelation was in the heart of him who loved Him. In sense experience you contact an object in space: in mystical experience you contact the Divine Life in the heart within. In this experience the heart transcends time and space and matter and machanism. This experience, oftener than not, cometh not in din and roar, in storm and thunder, but in a voice of stillness.

One of her companions said of her that Rabia prayed all night. she had but an interval of light sleep in her place of prayer when the day was about to dawn. Then, waking up, she would say:-

O my soul !
How long ?
How long wilt thou sleep ?
And how often wilt thou wake ?
Death is at the door:
And soon will the body sleep
A sleep that will no waking know
Untill the trumpet-call
Of the Day of Resurrection !

A companion asked Rabia:- "Is there a thing you would like to eat?"

Rabia said:- "You know I wish to eat dates. For ten years have I lived here: dates are plenty here. But I have not yet eaten a single date. Why? I am a servant of the one Master. The desire of the servant matters little. I can but eat or have what the Beloved wills for me!"

Rabia, indeed, had renounced everything to God. Not one thing could she call her own. Nothing belonged to her. All belonged to her Beloved. she too, was not her own but entirely His.

When asked:- "You speak of God: you worship Him. Have you seen Him?" Rabia answered:-"If I see Him not, how can I worship Him? But the Beloved cannot be weighed in words!"

Filled to overflowing was Rabia's heart with love. And to the worst of sinners she gave the love of her gentle heart.

One day she was asked:- "Don't you regard Satan as your enemy?"

Rabia gently answered:- "In my heart is limitless love for my Beloved: and I find there is not an empty corner in my heart for enmity to anyone or desire to fight anyone. By God's grace there is not one whom I may regard as my enemy!"

[8]

A mystic whose name is closely associated with that of Rabia was Hasan-al-Basri. Both were ascetics. Both represented early Sufism. A Muslim writer of note said the following of Hasan:-

Hasan was among the shining stars in learning, asceticism, virtue and devotion to God.

Hasan was noted, also for his jurisprudence and rhetoric and knowledge of the Divine things.

He was, also, a noted preacher: his sermons touched all hearts.

Hasan preached every Friday and Rabia went regularly to listen to him. He preached what he and Rabia practised in life,-renunciation. Many looked up to him as their *pir* or religious leader. His memory is still fragrant in Islam.

Like John the Baptist, who preached in another age and another country, Hasan asked his hearers to repent. He said:-

Repent ! Repent ! Repent !
This life and its pleasures are transient, passing !
Repent ! Repent ! Repent !

Great was his reverence for Rabia. One day, she was very late in coming. Hasan waited until she came. One of those present at the meeting asked him:-"Sir! why did you wait for Rabia?" Hasan answered:-'Whatever light shineth in my words cometh to me from the heart of Rabia."

We are told that Hasan hearing one day, of a man who said he would be happy if, even after a thousand years in Hell, he would be saved in the end, Hasan burst into tears!

They asked Hasan:-"Why do you weep, O preacher of the Word of God?"

He answered briefly:-"O, that I, too, might say like that man:-I shall be God's at last and shall be saved in the end!

Again and again, Hasan said with tears in his eyes:-"Alas! I am like a man who is in the sea with an old, broken boat,-trembling!"

Like Rabia, Hasan emphasised the thought that "the root of religion was abstinence." Again and again, he sounded the note:-

Restrain ! Restrain !
Restrain your carnal desires !
And remember God !

One day, Hasan asked Rabia:-"Tell me how you attained to this spiritual height."

Rabia answered:-"I know not where I stand: I only know that I did but one thing, friend! I scattered all I received."

Yes,- Rabia realised that life was given not to hoard but to scatter in the service of her Beloved.

One day, Hasan asked Rabia:-"Tell me what is God." Rabia said:-

He is as He is !
And you know it:
I think of Him in two ways thus:-
I think of Him as arupa and as amapa:
Arupa is He, for He hath no form !
Amapa is He, for He is Infinite, Measureless !

So thought, too, the great Sufi, Bayazid, when he compared God to the Sea that rolls on, unexhausted and unlimited Bayazid said:-"God is an unfathomable ocean!"

"Don't you desire Paradise?" Rabia was asked.

And she answered:-"It is the Lord of the House I need: what have I to do with the House?"

Speaking, one day, to hic congregation concerning the Way to Gog, Hasan said:-

Blessed is he who needs nothing, for he wiii have all !
Blessed is he who is a lover of solitude, for he will find peace !
Blessed is he who treads under his teet the lusts of the flesh, for he will be free !
Blessed is he who learns to endure, for he will have joy in Eternity !
Blessed is he who spends the night awake, for he listens to the voice that is deathless !
Blessed is he who forgets not God at night while the tears flow down his cheeks: for he will be accepted of the Lord !

As I read these beautiful words of Hasan, I say to myself:- "Is there not in them a moving picture of Rabia.-a lover of the Beloved?"

[9]

A companion asked Rabia:- "What is wisdom?'

Rabia said:-"True wisdom is knowledge of God: and the secret of knowledge is surrender to the Will Divine."

A friend asked her:- "Who among men is truly great?"

And Rabia answered:-"He who has achieved four things. (1) He who has purified his heart. (2) He who with the purified heart has learnt to pray to God. (3) He who hath risen to that true prayer which surrenders all to Him in spirit of *tawakul*, believing that 'He will take the best care of me'. And (4) he who is absorbed in meditation on Him and in singing His Name."

"Whence are you come?" they asked her

And she said:-"From the Other Shore!"

They asked her again:-"Whither are you going?"

She replied:-"To the Other Shorel!"

"If a man possessed the whole world," they asked, "would he not be immeasurably rich?"

Rabia answered:-"how could he be rich? The whole world would not make him wealthy: for the riches of the world perish and pass away."

"What do you desire?"Sufyan asked her.

Rabia answered:- "I am a servant: what has a servant to do with desires? If I ask for anything which my Lord does not will, then, indeed, I am an atheist, an unbeliever! If, indeed, I would be His servant, I should will only what He, my Divine Master, wills!"

A friend said to her:-"Rabia! you are ill:much have you suffered. Why don't you pray to God for relief from illness?"

Rabia answered:-"O friend! know you not who it is who wills this suffering for me? Is it not God who wills it?"

There was but one prayer in Rabia's heart, day and night:-"O God! My God! Thy Will be done!"

Malik Dinar was a Sufi: he was deeply pained to find that Rabia spent her days in poverty. He met her, one day, and said to her:- "permit me, Rabia! to ask my rich friends to relieve your poverty."

Rabia looked at Malik Dinar and said:-

> Your friends are rich. is it not true that He,-the One Lord,-gives daily bread alike to them and to me?
>
> Do you think He will ever forget the poor because they are poor, or remember the rich because they are rich?
>
> Does He not know my state?
>
> Why, then, should you remind Him that I am poor?
>
> Let us will what He wills and we shall be happy!

"Whence is Love?" they asked her, "and whither does it go?"

Rabia answered:-"Love cometh from Eternity: and love is a pilgrim to Eternity!"

Someone asked her:-"Don't you, sometimes, have a feeling of aversion to sinners?"

Rabia said:- "Love to God has, by His grace, so possessed me, that in my heart there is no room for aversion or hate to anyone."

"What is your hope?" they asked her.

She said:-

> *My hope is that my aspiration may be fulfilled.*
> *My aspiration is Union with Him.*
> *It is the goal of my Desire !*

Once she fell ill: in her heart was deep longing for God: and in a moment of inward pain she exclaimed:-"The healing of my wound is union with the Friend!"

A friend asked her:—"How may we know that God is well-pleased with His servant?"

Rabia said:—"When the servant greets 'suffering' as a gift from Him even as he would greet what he regards as 'good,'—regarding both pain and pleasure as messengers of God."

A friend asked her:—"What is the deepest need of the life of him who is in quest of God?"

Rabia said:—"He who would walk the Way needs neither eyes to see, nor tongue to tell. What he needs is a pure heart. So strive for purity. Then will your consciousness awake and you will no longer fall into the slumber of the senses when the mind is truly awakened, it serves as a true`friend: then, indeed, you need no other friend."

Her companion asked her:—"What is meant by the awakened mind?"

Rabia answered:—"One mark of the awakened mind is that it is centred in God and will not wanter after any thing else. The mind that is absorbed in the service of the One hath craving for nothing else."

Rabia had an "awakened mind:" and she had an "illuminated heart." Therefore was her life rich in the mystical element of love and adoration. Her "Sayings," as of Sri Ramakrishna's in our days, was love.

[10]

A Czech historian makes a suggestive distinction between "civilization" and "culture." Civilization, he says, is everything bequeathed to us by the past: but culture, he points out, is our activity in and upon this "inheritance". He points out, further, that we should so regulate our life that there should be no conflict between our "inheritance" and our "activity."

In India there is, alas! a conflict, a destructive conflict between the two. Our "inheritance" is spiritual: our "activity" is dominated by technical ideals. The conflict continues to grow. We tread the barren path of limitation, and our lives are becoming more and more shrunken, while we talk of economic "progress" and "efficiency."

Under the influence of the machine, man is in process of dehumanising himself: and we see how nations fight one with the other! We cry with the Poet:—"Alas! what man has made of man!" A great French thinker of our day, Marcel, deplores that we live in a "broken world:" and I recall the words of a mystic of Iran:—

Homeless am I, O Lord!
Whither shall I turn ?
A wanderer am I, O Lord!
Whither Shall I turn ?
I come, driven from every threshold:
And if Thy door, too, be closed.
Whither shall I turn ?
Faint are my limbs
And feeble is my strength,
And my heart is fearful, Lord!
Whither shall I turn ?

Blessed are they who live
In sight of Thee!
Who speak with Thee
And dwell with Thee, O Lord!
Humbly would I sit at the Feet
Of those who are dear to Thee!

Drunk, alas! with pleasure is this age:
In this drunken age
Thou art our Faith!
Helpless are we

And weak are our hands and feet !
How can we reach Thee ?
Thou art our Faith !
Christians or Muslims,
Hindus or Zarathustrians,
Whatever our country, colour or creed,
*Thou art our Faith !**

In these words is the deepest cry, too, of Rabia's heart. She regarded herself as a devotee of all Prophets, all Saints, all Silent Mystics: for "all come from Thee," she said.

Need I add that Rabia's "Prayers," too are most suggestive, in this connection:—

O God !
My God !
I have but one desire,—
To chant Thy Name
And to remember Thee
Above all the things of the earth.
And this, too, is the aspiration of my Heart
That I should, here and in the world beyond this world,
Meet Thee, face to face,
And only chant:—"Thy Will be done !"

* * *

O my Joy !
The desire of my Heart !
O my Friend,
My Life and my Love !
My Beloved !
If only Thou
Be well pleased with me,
Then am I happy, indeed,
Beyond all measure,
Happy at Thy Holy Feet !

---

*The poem is given here, with slight modifications.

Yet another prayer, very brief, very beautiful. I never read it but my eyes are touched with tears. This little prayer I am tempted to quote as I close:—

O God !
My God !
The stars are shining !
And the eyes of men
Are in slumber closed !
And kings have shut their doors
And every lover is alone
With his Beloved.
And here Am I
Alone with Thee.
Alone with the Beloved !

St. Francis: The Selfless

[1]

IN THE YEAR 1226, on October 4, Francis passed on, blessing all his brethren, saying to them:—"Farewell, my children! abide in the fear of the Lord and ever persevere therein!"

He was in the forty-fifth year of his life. He had asked to be buried on a hill on which it was customary to execute criminals: but this desire of the saint could not be fulfilled. His holy body was laid to rest in the Church of St. George. A few years later, his remains were translated to their new resting-place.

A moving, little legend tells us that he was born in a stable, transformed now into a chapel,—the Chapel of the "Little Saint Francis:" and over its door may still be read the words:—

> This chapel has been the stable of ox and of ass:
>
> In which was born Francis, the wonder of the world.

In a village, named Assisi, stands this chapel: Assisi is, today, a place of pilgrimage. When Francis learns that his end is near, he wishes to be taken to Assisi: and, as the litter in which they carry the saint approaches Assisi, citizens flock with cries of joy to meet the man they once had stoned! There, when the doctor tells him that his sickness is incurable and that he soon must die, he raises his hands in reverence to the Lord, his eyes beaming bright, and he exclaims:—"Welcome! my Sister Death!" And he spends the night singing. On the last day he blesses Assis. To this dear disciple, Clare, he sends a tender message:—"Put aside all sorrow and sadness." And he breathes his last, singing the following words from the Psalm:—"Bring my soul out of prison that I may praise Thy Name!"

Francis loved all birds but, above all, the lark. To him the lark was a symbol of humility, for she would gladly go by the way to find a few grains of corn, even among the dung, and eat them. He addressed the lark as his sister. On the last day of his life, two larks came from their grove,—a chronicler says,—to bid farewell to

Francis. And Francis smiled, then gently murmured:— "My larks sing for me: praised be my Lord!"

Like Buddha and Mahavir, like Kabir and Nanak, life all the saints and seers of India, Francis felt himself to be a brother of all creatures,—of birds and animals and plants, of elements and stars and streams. Dear to him were sparrows and doves, flowers and trees,—as members of his own Order!

[2]

Meditating on him,—his wonderful life and his illuminating "Sayings",—I have asked myself, again and again:—"Who is he?"

He remainds me of some of the *rishis* (seers) of India, some of the *fakirs* (renouncers) and *dervishes* (contemplatives) of the East.

Francis renounces everything: he possesses nothing: he is Christ-possessed. In poverty is his joy, for his Master, Jesus, he knows, was poor. Francis shows the beauty and fascination of the simple life. He is, he says, betrothed to "Lady Poverty": he rejoices in the betrothal. His very soul sings in the words:—"Poverty is the virtue which makes the soul, while still restrained on earth, converse with the angels in heaven."

Brought up as a prince, he flings away riches. As a true disciple of Christ he reflects, by day and night, the radiance of holy poverty. At night he sleeps on the ground and has under him nothing but a little straw. He has discarded all pillows. A testimony to this is given us in the words of dignitary of his Church, who afterwards became Pope Gregory. Looking at the Franciscan brethren, as they slept at night, Gregory wept, saying:—"Look you here, where the brethren sleep, while we, unworthy ones, do make use of so many superfluities."

Francis moves out from place to place: he has no money in his pocket. Money is a burden! He goes out to preach with light steps, with joy in his heart. He sweeps out the churches with a broom, his anxiety being to keep the churches clean. He washes dishes in other people's kitchens: he begs bread from door to door: but he is cheerful, happy: there is a song on his lips.

He believes in the sanctity of manual labour and he sets an example to others by toiling with his hands. "Idleness," he says again and again, "is the enemy of the soul. The servants of God must always be either at prayer or employed in doing some good work."

In the Cross is his perfect joy. Therefore, he kisses the lepers and is happy to be a servant of the poor. "Rejoice," he says, "when you converse with persons who are mean and despised by the world." His is no hunger-born socialism: his is a socialism of the Spirit: it is sung in rapturous songs and lived, even today, by some of the *dervishes* and *fakirs* of the East. "When you see a poor man," says Francis, "you should remember in whose name he came, that of of Christ, who took upon himself our poverty and our infirmity. This man's poverty and infirmity is for us, as it were, a mirror wherein we can gaze and devoutly consider the poverty and infirmity of our Lord Jesus Christ."

One day, indeed, when a poor man asked an alms of Francis, the saint, in a temporary lapse, forgot his usual custom and passed by the poor man unheeded. But speedily, Francis recollected himself, ran after the poor man, and liberally relieved his wants. That very day, Francis made a solemn promise to God that he would never again refuse an alms to any poor man who would ask it of him for the love of God. And this promise, we may be sure, Francis faithfuly kept till the day of his death.

Francis meets, one day, a poor man laden with a heavy burden: Francis lifts the load on his own shoulders and carries it for him. One other day, Francis, meeting a poor man, puts off his own mantle and gives it to him, saying:—"This mantle was with me but as a loan until such time as I should find one poorer than myself."

Francis washes the feet of the lepers and cleanses their wounds. One day, a leper meets him: he empties his purse in the leper's hand. Francis would not send away even the robbers. He would be like the sun that giveth its light to the just and the unjust. Some robbers break into one of his "retreats," and are driven away by the guardian of the place. Francis learns of it and immediately sends them the bread prepared for his own meals and a gentle message of love: and they come and fall down at his feet!

In a period, smitten with scramble for money and power, Francis shows the Way of a New Life. It is the way of simplicity. "Pure and holy simplicity," he says, "confounds the wisdom of this world, and the wisdom of the flesh."

[3]

A little spare figure, a thin worn-out body, Francis is physical so frail and weak, but his eyes are so sweet and bright! They shine with the light of love. Mournfulness and melancholy are not in his creed of life. "To the devil," he says, "belongs to be sad, but to us ever to be glad and rejoice in the Lord," Francis believes in the gospel of spiritual cheerfulness. From time to time, he suddenly breaks forth into a song of joy, singing of his Lord and Master, Jesus. We read that the saint, meeting one day a disciple who has a sad face rebukes him, saying:— "Why this outward grief and sadness? Let it be between you and God. But before me and others strive to be cheerful. Remember, it is not seemly that a servant of God should show a sad and troubled face before his brethren."

Bravely does Francis battle with his body, becoming more and more rigid in controlling himself, his thoughts and conduct, more and more rigid in training his body, his mind and his heart in purity: but never does he lose his spiritual cheerfulness. To discipline his body he often plunges in winter-time into a pit of ice and snow, but he never surrenders his gladness of spirit. One day, as Francis is assailed by a violent temptation, he puts off his clothes and beats himself with a cord. Even then he does not lose his sense of humour. He says, speaking to his body:—Brother Ass! thus dost thou deserve to be treated, thus to be beaten." What tremendous *tapasya* (self-restraint, self-chastisement) he goes through, this *fakir* of Christ, until he conquers the flesh! And with love and joy in his heart, he gives blessings to everyone. "The Lord give thee peace!"—this is his salutation to every one who meets him. "Peace to all beings!"—'*'Shanti'*—was the blessing breathed out by the *rishis* of India.

A *fakir* is a pilgrim: and as a pilgrim, Francis goes through the world, "taking nothing with him but Christ crucified," and for the sake of Christ putting up with the world's insult and dishonour. One day, certain robbers fall upon Francis, asking him who he is. Francis says:—"I am the herald of the great King of Heaven." The robbers fall on him with fury, and strike him with blow after blow, and then cast him into a ditch, filled with snow, saying:—"Lie thou into the ditch, thou herad of nothing, yet thou callest thyself a herald of God!" But Francis minds it not. In the ditch itself Francis goes on singing the praises of the Lord with joy and gladness.

[4]

And is not Francis, the very picture of humility? A disciple asks him:—

Why is it that all the world cometh after thee?
Why is it that everybody desireth to see thee?
And to hear and to obey thee?
Thou art not handsome:
Thou art not a man of great knowledge.
Whence, then, comes it
That all the world runneth after thee?

And Francis, in deep humility, answereth thus:—

Brother! wouldst thou know indeed,
Why all the world runneth after me?
This comes to me, brother!
Because the eyes of Him, the most High,
Have not found among sinners
One more vile,
Nor more incompetent,
Nor; indeed, a greater sinner than I.
And, therefore, to do His wonderful work,
God hath not found on earth
A creature idler and more foolish than I.
So it is, brother!
That he hath chosen me
To confound the nobility and the grandeur,
The strength and beauty,
The wisdom and virtue of the world,

That all men may know
That all virtue and all goodness
Cometh of God
And not of any creature!

[5]

Like St. John, Francis,—who indeed was first named John by his mother,—is filled with the love of God. Francis, indeed, could never hear the words, "the love of God," without passing through a tremendous transformation. As soon as he heard the words, "the love of God," he was stirred, he was inflamed; he was filled with a strange feeling, as though someone was touching the inner chord of his heart. In one of his utterances, we have the following remarkable words:-

All my will is burnt up with love,
Is united to love,
Is transformed into love,
Is consumed and consecrated by love.
Neither the fire nor the sword
Shall separate me from love.
Suffering and death never may rise
To the heights to which love doth lure me on.
Outside this mystic union with love,
All created things are restless:
By love the soul is raised,
Is exalted, elevated, above everything!

Like Sri Chaitanya, like Baba Farid and Shams Tabriz and Jalalu'l-Din Rumi, like Baba Nanak and Abdul Latif and other *dervishes* of the east, Francis sings continually of the immeasurable Love of God. And his words, to quote Celano, "are like fire penetrating the heart." It is the fire of love. And there comes a time when the common people greet this *fakir* as a prince among men. When he reaches a city or a town, they ring the bells and they run to meet him and wave green branches, and children clap their hands and sing in sheer joy.

He is not an ascetic,—cold, blunt, indifferent to life. He is not a reformer, out to ship men into goodness. He is not a socialist, swayed by a creed of class-conflict. He is a witness of Love. His songs and sermons reveal him as an apostle of Love. Listen to his words:—

> With all thy heart love the love which loves thee, love the Love which desires thee, and has created thee to draw thee wholly to Himself!

He does not forget that the rich, too, must be treated as brothers. "Do not judge," he says, "nor despise the rich, who live at ease and who wear fine clothes, for God is their Saviour as well as ours. We ought to honour them as our brothers, for we all have the same Creator." Not class-conflict, not hate, not violence, but peace is his watchword. "Go, preach peace to men!" he says.

[6]

In love and utter simplicity, Francis mingles with the poor. He admits no one to his Order who will not strip himself of all things, retaining nothing for himself. Francis believes profoundly in the teaching of his Master, "Go and sell all thou hast and give to the poor!"

A peasant meets Francis, saying to him:—"O saint of God! I long to serve God. Blessed am I to have met you! Accept me in you Brotherhood, and tell me what I should do to please you."

Francis says to him:—"Brother! if you will, indeed, be of my company and my interior life, go part with all your goods and give them to the poor."

Francis understands what a blessing it is to belong to the brotherhood of the poor. "It were a quicker journey to God from a hut," he says, "than from a palace." And poorer and purer than the "poor" are birds and animals. How much Francis loves them!

A youth has caught a number of turtle-doves and is taking them to market. He meets Francis on the way. "I pray thee, give me these gentle birds," says the saint. The good youth gives them all. And Francis receives them into his bosom, talks to them tenderly, and builds nests for them all.

A fisherman brings to Francis a water-fowl. Francis accepts the bird, then opens his hands to let it fly away. Another fisherman bringes to him a great fish alive. Francis puts it back into the water of the lake. He speaks to swallows: he preaches to birds.

So great was St. Francis' love for the larks and other birds that he, on one occasion, said in tender, touching words:—"How happy would I feel if all the mayors of the cities and all the lords of the castles and towns would solemnly promise every year on the day, sacred as the birthday of our Lord, to induce their men to do one thing,—to throw their wheat and their grain along the roads beyond the cities and walled towns so that our sisters, the larks and other birds, may have plenty to eat!"

His love tamed even a wolf: the "good wolf of Gubbio" they called the "little brother of St. Francis." Animals respond to love: but we, alas! torture them. "By what cries of pain," writes Countess Caesaresco, "by what looks of love have not beasts told men that they *thought*!" "Behold the animals! There is not one," writes Edward Carpenter, "but the human soul lurks within it, fulfilling its destiny as surely as within you!" The "God of the granite and the rose" is, also, "the soul of the sparrow and the bee" and the spirit of the tender goat and the mild cow and lamb.

The nations, alas! are wandering today in a "jungle" of "civilisation." The nations love violence: they trample upon the great vision of the One Life in all. Modern civilisation is baptized in blood. Even India is forgetting her ancient vision of reverence for life. I have heard "educated" Indians speak, echoing the words of some Western books, of "humane" slaughter! As well might we speak of "humane" murder! Stop *all* slaughter, brother!

St. Francis was a brother of all animals, a brother of life, a brother of all creatures. In his heart he communed with the Brotherhood of Life. An influence moved out of him, a strange, psychic influence: it enveloped others with the tenderness and love of his heart which felt for all creatures, human and sub-human.

He met, one day, a wood-cutter, chpping down a tree. To him, Francis spake:—"Brother! do not chop off the whole tree, but give it a chance to grow up again." And Francis offered him his food for the day.

Francis loved plants and flowers: when he saw flowers, he was filled with joy. Francis, like Buddha, embraced all creatures in love. Buddha carried on his shoulders a goat, which was being led to the sacrificial altar, and, meeting the king of the place, said:—"Sire! I offer myself as a sacrifice in the place of this poor, helpless, bleating goat." And the king was so moved that he released the goat. Francis blessed the wolf and, with the power of love, transformed the wolf into a mild animal.

[7]

Francis was a wanderer without house or home: this homeless wanderer found his home in Nature and in the hearts of all creatures. In his "Canticle of the Sun," he praises "Brother Sun," through whom God doth light us: the Sun, Francis says, is a living image of "my Lord, the Highest." And Francis praises the Moon and Stars as his "Sisters," the Wind as his "brother," Water as his "sister" and Fire as his "brother," through whom "Thou, O Lord, dost illuminate the night!" And Francis praises the Lord through "Mother Earth, Rich in Fruits and coloured flowers and grasses."

Remarkable is his "Canticle of the Sun." It shows that the heart of the saint was filled, through and through, with cosmic emotion for Nature, for the Sun and the Moon and the Stars, for Fire and Water, for all the elements which are indeed emanations of the Lord, making the Universe a Temple of beauty and joy. St. Francis' "Canticle of the Sun" has reminded me, again and again, of Guru Nanak's invocation to the Lord of creation, called *arati.* Listen to the following words of St. Francis:—

> Most High, Omnipotent, Good Lord!
> To Thee be the praise,
> The glory, the honour and all benediction:
> To Thee alone, Most High, do they belong,
> And no man is worthy
> To name Thy Name!
>
> To Thee be praise
> In all Thy creatures, Lord!
> Praise be to Thee for Brother Sun!
> By him is the Earth illumined, day by day:

And radiant is he and bright.
With what splendour shineth he!
The Sun, indeed, is a symbol of Thee!

To Thee be praise
For Brother Fire, my Lord!
Thou dost by Fire
Illuminate night after night.
How noble is Brother Fire!
How beautiful!
How robust and strong!

To Thee be praise
For Sister Water, Lord!
How humble is she!
How useful, too!
Ever chaste is she,
Pure beyond compare!

To Thee be praise, my Lord!
For Sister Moon and Stars.
In heaven they shine:
How fair!
How clear!
How precious!

To Thee be praise
For Brother Wind, my Lord!
For Air and Clouds:
For times serene and stormy.
To Thee be praise forever!

To Thee be praise, my Lord!
For Mother Earth,
Who doth sustain and keep us,
And bringeth forth fruits
And coloured flowers and grass!

To Thee be praise, my Lord!
For those who pardon for Thy love,
Who bear infirmity and tribulation.
Blessed are they
Who will in peace endure:
For Thou, Most High,
Shall give unto them a crown!

To Thee be praise, O Lord!
For our Sister Bodily Death
From whom no man can escape.
Alas for them who die in mortal sin!
Blessed are they
Who are found in Thy Holy Will,
For the second death will not work them harm!

His feeling for Nature became for him a key to a new world of kinship and sympathy. Has it no message for the modern man? In India, in the long age, men lived in fellowship with all creatures, with all life. Creation was one Family in God! This vision of cosmic unity inspired the ancient *rishi*, when he sang:—"*Ishavasyam sarvam idam*!" "All that is, is a vesture of the Lord!" In this message of unity with flower and field, with bird and animal, there is, methinks, a hope for mankind.

Leibniz, the great French philosopher, was a seer. He had the beautiful idea, the profound vision, that life on earth had three manifestations. Life sleeps in plants: life dreams in animals: life wakes in man. Yes,—life is animals. Bruno, one of the great minds of the middle Ages, pointedly said:—"Among horses, elephants and dogs, there are single individuals which appear to have almost the understanding of man."

Francis became the great awakener of his age. A new awakening is the world's piteous need, today. New sons and daughters of Krishna and Buddha, or Mahavir and Francis, are needed, today, to reveal anew the beauty of reverence for life,—sons and daughters, who would, renouncing eminence and honours, greed and greatness, be among the servants of animals and humanity.

[8]

Shams Tabriz, the *dervish*, meets Jalalu'l-Din Rumi on the bank of a river, poring over his books. The *dervish* throws the scholar's books into the river and says:—"Close these books: open thou the Scripture of the Heart!" The way to it is love. So have the *dervishes* of the East taught, age after age. So teaches St. Francis. He says:—

> A man has as much knowledge as he does deeds; he who relies upon book-learning, in the day of sorrow and battle, will find his hands empty....Many there are who are fain to exalt themselves unto knowledge, but he will be blessed who maketh his mind to be barren for the love of God.

Not book-learning, but wisdom of the heart is the great treasure of life. This makes Francis an extraordinary psychic. He develops telepathic powers, easily reading the thoughts of others: his powers of suggestion and personal magnetism multiply: he hears voices speaking to him from the crucifix: his healing power increases. Many poor persons "possessed" and "out of mind" are brought back to tranquillity by his healing touch. A woman regains sight on being blessed by Francis. Another woman's withered hands recover vitality at the touch of the saint.

An old chronicle calls him an "angelic man." Never did he descend to work and the service of the poor and lowly without having first lifted up his heart to God to receive of Him the strength and the light he needed for work amid the tumult of multitudes. He would first purify his spirit from any dust which might have clung to him in his contact with men. Purified and illumined by God, in silence, he descended to the plane of activity and service. Again and again, he would at night rise from his bed and, raising his eyes and his hands to heaven, he would say, "My God! My God!" and he would repeat these words until morning, uttering but these two words, "My God! My God!" And again, when he saw that some of his disciples lived not as they should or sometimes spoke even to him words in irritation or anger, straightway would Francis go to prayer. And coming out of his silence-corner, he gave blessing to everyone, never saying, "so and so spoke to me thus" or "so and so did violate a rule of the Order." St. Francis was a man essentially of prayer: therefore was he a quiet man, a man of silence, one who breathed out his benedictions to everyone, even as the sun sends out its light to good and to evil alike.

Bare-footed and clad in a brown robe, he goes on his mission of help and healing, greeting every passer-by on the road:—"Brother! the Lord give you His Peace!" His wealth, his wisdom, his joy are in the Cross. And in all this wanderings, he bears in his heart the ringing words of his great Master:—"He that would save his life must lose it!"

His gentle, lovely figure hath ravished my heart: and I lift up my eyes to him, again and again, in this age of many creeds and much confusion. A new simplification of life is the need of civilisation. A simple message is what the world waits for. Hence the value of a new study of St. Francis. The Nations cannot escape him. His gaze has gone through them. It is the gaze of a God-intoxicated *fakir*. In him the Kingdom of Grace is come anew. Through him a new passion has passed into the life of man. Seven centuries and more have not exhausted this new passion, this new vision of the Cross. In Francis, the *fakir*, I behold the Face of Christ!

Guru Nanak : A Prophet Of The People

THE LIFE OF Guru Nanak was one continuous *yagna*,—sacrifice to God. Some of the Gurus died martyrs: Guru Nanak was born a martyr to the One Eternal Mystery,—God! Nanak travelled to many parts of India and Asia: he went, I am told, as far as the Russian borderland. Every travel of Nanak was a *yagna*,—an offering,—to the One God of all nations, all races, all religions.

His life, from beginning to end, taught this one truth that every man,—no matter what his creed or country,—was, in essence, a Nanak. Is not every man illuminated with the one Light Divine, and meant to be an offering to the *Akal Purukha* (the Eternal One) in the service of love? So let the *bhaktas* see Nanak not once but again and again,—in all men, in all creation.

Nanak's life opened an era in the history of India and Asia,—in the history of humanity. He was a Prophet, a Seer and a Saint. India's history is, to me, incomprehensible without Nanak. He was centuries ahead of his age. He realised, what the world's statesmen have not yet realised, that all men are one, that, therefore, Hindu-Muslim conflicts and all conflicts of "creeds" and "classes" and nations are born of "illusion." So Guru Nanak stood for the weak and the poor, for the men who toiled and strove for truth. He realised that more than food and fire, men's need was sympathy and brotherhood.

He blessed the Hindu and the Muslim. One of his dearest disciples was the Muslim singer, Mardana,—he who accompanied the Guru as, in the blue garb of a Muslim pilgrim, and carrying a staff, a cup and a praying carpet, the Guru moved out on his travels to the North and the South, to East and West. Guru Nanak called Mardana, "*bhai*." Indeed, this Muslim singer was the Guru's first *bhai* (brother).

The Guru gave his love the the maimed and the halt, to the hungry and the blind. "Be my brother," says a Nazi proverb, "or I will bash your head in." How superior to the Nazi and Communist conception of brother-hood was the vision of the Guru, who said:—"My brother art thou, and I shall be thy servant in the dust and the dirt of the earth, for we all belong to the Family of Him who is the One Father of all!"

And he was so humble! His face radiated humility and love. In the centuries that have followed his advent and seen the rise and fall of kingdoms in this ancient land. I have known none greater than his humble prophet and saint. This radiant and transfigured Son of God has been, for fifty years and more, a leader of my thought and life.

"I Belong To No Sect !"

At rare intervals in history doth appear a man like Nanak. He is attuned from the beginning of his days to cosmic forces and the Cosmic Will: he hears vioces and he sees visions in waking life and in dreams. His values of life are not the values of the world. Others value money, honours, earthly goods: he values the invisible Treasure of the Eternal. He fears not the power of man: he fears not death: for he hath looked into the radiant Face of Life. He hath learnt to renounce the goods of time and all ambition and all reputation. He hateth none, and he harmeth none: for to him every creature,—human and sub-human,—is a brother, a sister in the one Kingdom of Life, and even atoms are illuminated with the One Light: every planet and every sun and every star is flooded with love in the one Sea of Life!

The Hindus of Sind are followers of this one Incomparable Man, this one Inspired and Illuminated Prophet,—Nanak Shah. He adored the One. This One, Nanak taught, was above all the gods, all the forces of Nature: this One, said Nanak, is He "whose Name is True: repeat His Name,—the True One! In the beginning was He: the True One was in the primal age: the True One is: the True One was as the True One shall be for aye!"

In his answers to the questions put to him by the *Maulvis,*—the priests,—at Mecca, he bore witness to his faith which was different, at once from the Islam of the Mullah and the Hinduism of the Pundit. Nanak said:—

> To whom shall I go to know of Thee, my God? Thou art the greatest of the great: and great is Thy Word. Veiled is Thy greatness from men and they depart in pride, in the vanity of little knowledge!
>
> I have searched through and through the four Vedas and the four Books of the Mussulman; but the Illimitable escapes them and they are dumb, speechless in the presence of the Mystery of the Infinite.
>
> This be my faith,—saith Nanak, the servant of all,—to adore the One Mystery and to do good to all.

So when the high priest of Baghdad said to him, "Tell me to what sect thou dost belong," Nanak said:—

> I belong to no sect:
> A adore but One God!
> And I see Him in the Earth below
> And the Heavens above
> And in all directions!

Simplify !

Nanak's life is like a bell with many echoes. The one note it sounds, again and again, is the note of simplicity. The simplicity of Nanak will draw to him, more and more, the youths of Asia and the West. And this man of simplicity is a man of sacrifice. His life is religion,—not a theory, a philosophy, a creed, the programme of a party or a church. His convictions come from action and contemplation, not information or scholarship. Blessed is the nation that has such men to inspire and lead. If India lies prostrate today,—the bulk of her people hungry and in rags,—it is because her statemen lack the inspiration of the simple, spiritual life.

Simple was Nanak in food and dress: and simple was the

message he gave to the people. At Brindaban, he saw, with sadness in his heart, crowds of men and women, singing and dancing. Krishna's name was on their lips but in their hearts, alas! was darkness,—the darkness of "desire," *trisna*. And Nanak sang on the spot a simple song: and how simple was its message to the people!

> "Give up," said Nanak, "desire, craving!
>
> "Give up the *tapasyas*, the penances which punish the body and do not purify the heart!
>
> "Seek the grace of the Lord!
>
> "He asketh of you good deeds and *Harikirtan*. Sing His Name!
>
> "With truth and resignation as your cymbals, sing His Name in chorus:
>
> "And keep time in the true dance,
>
> "Which is the dance of humility."

So, at Hardwar, when he sees the *bairagis* and *sanyasins* quarelling, one with the other, for honours and greatness, Guru Nanak sings a simple Song, charged with a message they all understand:—

> Your colour your clothes but, alas! you walk not in humility!
>
> You forget the Word (*Nam*) and so, alas! you gamble away your soul for a trifle of earthly honour!
>
> Be ye householders or *sanyasins* or *yogis*: blessed among you are the simple who ever dwell at the feet of the Lord in Love.

Religion Of Life

One meaning of the word "Nanak," I am told, is "fire." Nanak was illuminated by the Divine Fire. For him God was enough: with God he communed,—with God and God's Angels. Utterly fused in him was the ego: the miracle of transfiguration was made manifest in his life, again and again, since the day he plunged for bath in the

Ravi and heard the voice of the *Akal Purukha*:—"Nanak! I give unto thee the Word! Go forth and proclaim It among the Nations."

Since that blessed day we see Nanak enraptured, again and again, in an ecstasy of "*Nama,"—the* "*Sat Nama*." God has called Nanak out from the usual run of men: God hath called Nanak to a special task, and every moment of his life is henceforth centred round the Innermost Flame of *Sat Nama*,—the Word! And as this Central Flame of the Soul burns brighter and brighter, Nanak comes nearer and nearer to God: Nanak rises ever up and up to God's Holiness: and the nearer Nanak comes to Holiness, the deeper grows within him the feeling of insufficiency, the feeling of humility. The nearer Nanak comes to God in the pursuit of Truth and Perfection, the deeper he sinks into nothingness. "Nearer my God, to Thee!"—is Nanak's aspiration, and the nearer he comes to God, the more radiant is he, for he grows in the power to reveal the veiled Mystery to other men.

The secret of his nearness is love of God and self-sacrificing love for fellow-men. He has gazed at the beauteous face of God: and on him falls a ray of God's radiant holiness: and his life becomes magnetic: as he travels from place to place a strange influence streams out of him. In his nearness to God is the secret of Nanak's power of attraction over the hearts and lives of men and women. Nanak transmits his influence in his travels, far and wide.

Nanak's influence has not waned but has grown, as centuries have gone. Nanak is, today, a flaming symbol. Through Nanak, as through the great Saints, God gives continuous witness of Himself, God renews perpetually the life of man. And when I read of the brave, heroic Khalsas moving in a procession of pilgrims to the Dera Sahib,—a territory now belonging to Pakistan,—or of the dauntless Sikh leader serenely meditating on the *Guru Bani* during his trial in the court of law, I say to myself:—"Is not Guru Nanak still an active force today, a dynamic vitality to many men and women, a fire to his chosen few,—a fire which never is extinguished?"

I read the story of Guru-Ka-Bagh with tear-touched eyes and ask:—"Is not Guru Nanak a reality to not a few even in the twentieth century?" A band of a hundred Akalis in black turbans march from Amritsar, having taken the vow at the Golden Temple that they will die for the Guru but will do no violence by word or deed. They march to the birth-place of the Guru,—to "Nankana Sahib." They march as pilgrims, as worshippers, and in silence they sit on an open plot of ground. Their lips move in prayer to the Guru, even as the police begin their cruel beating. A police officer strikes with his brass-bound *lathi* at the collar-bone of a praying Akali Sikh: he rolls over the ground, his lips move in prayer: slowly he gets up again: the brass-bound club falls on him again: he prays on to the Guru without a word of violence. Blessed are the meek! He is struck, again and again: he resists not the brutal blows: he bears them bravely, until he falls down, unconscious, and is taken up by the brave ambulance volunteers. Other Akali Sikhs, too, behave as does this brave one: they have served in the Army: they have fought in Flanders and France, in Mesopotamia and East Africa: but this time they have taken a vow that they will be silent and peaceful: and blow after blow they endure in the spirit of prayer: they remember the Guru: they commune with the spirit of Nanak: they will not retaliate: the Guru is to them a living reality! Blow after blow falls on them: they continue to sing in silence the *Nama*: they commune with the Word Eternal. Does not Nanak say in his great hymn, the *Japji*?

> In communion with the "Word," the "Nama,"
> Rise superior to all shocks of the world,
> Nor fear the dreaded angel of Death!
> For, listening to the *Nama*, the "Word,"
> Thou art with wisdom armed!
> And departing, thou guest openly
> With a wreath of laurels crowned!

In another place, Nanak says:—

> None is mine enemy,
> And none to me a stranger is!
> Saith Nanak, servant of all:—
> "All, all are my brethren in the One Beloved!"

Yes,—Nanak saw all as his "brethren in the One Beloved." So his words went home to all. To a Muslim teacher, Nanak said:—

Make compassion thy mosque,
And sincerity thy prayer-carpet,
And justice thy *Koran*:
So mayst thou be a true Mussulman!
And again:—

Five be thy prayers:—
The first is truth.
The second is righteousness,
The third is charity,
The fourth is pure aspiration,
And the fifth is the praise and glory of God!
And let deeds of service
Be thy creed, O brother!
So mayst thou be a true Mussulman!

To a farmer, the Guru said:—

Let thy body be the field:
And sow in it the seed of good deeds:
And irrigate the field with God's Name:
And let thy heart cultivate:
So will God germinate in thy heart:
So wilt thou achieve liberation.

To a shopkeeper, the Guru said:—

Life is frail: let this knowledge be thy shop: and let thy stock-in-trade be the Word of God! And make prayer and meditation thy vessels, and fill them with the *Nama*,—the Word of God!

To a soldier, the Guru said:—

Let thy horse be honesty: and put on the armour of continenece: and let truth be thy sword and shield!

And again:—

Let thy daily food be meekness!
And never forget that all force is oppression:
And remember, too, that justice is pure!

To a householder, the Guru said:—

In thy heart is God: why seek Him elsewhere?
Truth is higher than everything:
But higher still is true living.
Not in repeating *mantras* is religion.
He who sees the One in all is religious.
Religion is not in wandering to tombs.
Nor to places of cremation!
Religion is not in exterior postures,—*asanas*,—of contemplation,
Religion is not making pilgrimages to foreign places,
Religion is not bathing in rivers or temple-baths!
He who abideth pure
Amidst the world's temptations,—
He hath known the spirit of Religion!

The emphasis of nanak is on the heart and on "golden deeds" of the heart. Nanak rose above philosophy and metaphysics, above rites and ceremonies, above creeds and conventions, above all nation-cults and all "race-gospels" to a vision of deeds of love. "God will not ask man," said Nanak, "of what race he is: He will but ask him, `What have you done?'" Deeds, not creeds, is what Nanak asks of his disciples. Nanak preached a Religion for which men would live,—a Religion which would shine in the lives of men, a Religion which would be a service of Life!

Many, today, have lost faith in religion because religion has been separated from life. Religion will come into its own when men will learn to live amicably and helpfully with their fellow-men. Nanak's vision of life embraced all countries, all religions, all races. Nanak taught the Unity of God and Brotherhood of man. Civilisation is sinking, for there is a lack of unity in our lives. Civilisation may be saved if life is built in the new synthesis which Nanak preached.

Spiritual Communism

In the Ravi river, Nanak plunges for a bath. It is a blessed bath. A Voice speaks to him in the music of the waters: and in the silence of his soul, he knows God by personal contact of the heart with the Harmony of the Eternal Self. Nanak realises that he is solitary,—a soul alone with God!

He comes out of the waters: his face shines with a strange, unearthly light. Nanak has had a vision of the Spirit whose Brightness fills the river, and fills the sun and stars and fills the temple of the heart.

Nanak realises his kinship with the village-folk, realises that, if he must travel to cities, he must go there as a spiritual physician to cure men and women of diseases of the soul, which the cities breed.

Nanak grows into a vision of spiritual communism. Nanak realises that he has nothing which does not, at the same time, belong to all, that his food and garments he must share with the poor, that the richest privilege of life is to share all you have all. In the great stress Nanak lays on fellowship and brotherhood, he reveals the secret of true spiritual communism.

Nanak looks on the poor and needy with new eyes of understanding and love: he sees the world lit up with the One Light, from end to end. "*Ishavasyam Sarvamidam*!" "All this is covered with the One, as with a garment!"—said a Rishi.

Nanak sees the world with new, radiant eyes. Nanak has glimpsed the beauty of the Kingdom of Heaven." Nanak takes upon himself the yoke of this Kingdom. Nanak prepares to go out to give to men and women, of diverse countries and faiths, the message of the One Father-Mother of all, and the One Brotherhood radiant with the light of simplicity of living, and adoration and love of the Divine.

A flame is in Nanak's heart: Nanak goes out among the nations to give them a message of the Flame. In the Chariot of Flame goes out the Great Lord.—the *Akal Purukha*,—to meet Man. He is a Pilgrim to his home in the Eternal Flame,—God. Man's way to God is the way of *yagna*, the way of sacrifice. In a Jewish scripture, we read:—

> Johanan, the Master, was riding on an ass. Eliezer was behind him. And Eliezer said to Johanan:—"Master! wilt thou give me leave to tell thee a thing which thou hast taught me?" "Yes," replied Johanan, "say it!" Forthwith, he dismounted from his ass, wrapped himself up in a garment and sat upon a stone beneath the olive tree. "Why, O Master, hast thou dismounted from thy ass?" asked Elizer. And Johanan replied:—"Is it possible that I will ride upon my ass at the moment when thou art expounding the Mysteries, and the Presence Divine is with us and the Angels are accompanying us?" Forthwith, Eliezer opened his talk on the Mysteries, and no sooner had he begun than fire came down from heaven and encompassed all the trees of the field which, with one accord, burst into song!

Guru Nanak sits in the shade of a tree: Mardana plays upon the *rabab*: does not a "flame" come down from heaven and encompass the tree? And does not the flame burst into a Song,—The Song of Guru Nanak? The Guru sits in silence, cleansed of all pride, lowly and meek, with a flame in his heart, and the flame burst into Song. In every word of Guru Nanak is humility: the Song is not for the haughty, but for the poor and pure in heart. And the way to purity is the culture of humility.

Guru Nanak goes out on his travels: Mardana is with him: yet not he alone. The Angels are with Nanak: for Angels, as a Jewish Rabbi says, "are created, day by day, from the stream of fire." From Nanak flows a "stream of fire." Guru Nanak's Song sings of the soul as a "bride" and of God as the "Bridegroom." Guru Nanak's Song is charged with the music of Bride and Bridegroom! Guru Nanak sings of spiritual marriage between the soul and God,—sings of a betrothal between the two.

"Save Thy People, O Lord !"

The Japji and many other songs of Guru Nanak have profound sayings, more precious than rubies and gold. Yet must we not regard Nanak as a metaphysician or a philosopher. I look up to him as one whose life was luminous with the light of the Spirit. The great thoughts of Guru Nanak spring from his simple heart. Not rational but symbolic thought is the secret of the beauty of Nanak's teaching.

In the *Japji* (the Guru's "Sermon of the Mount") is set forth, in symbols, the teaching that to know God and the Saints we must love them. None met God on the road of conception: only by love and devotion and self-dedication may a man enter into the way of true knowledge and realisation and truth.

Guru Nanak appeared at a time when India was invaded by dark forces. India's civilisation and the Aryan *dharma* were sinking: a new age of violence was arising in the midst of conflict and chaos. The soul of Guru Nanak cried out to God to save the People. Politicians could not: they were men who pushed their way to power, and placed their creed and their party above the people. Guru Nanak turned to no government for help; for he realised that governments just keep the ring to see that combat continues: governments cannot win peace.

At Saidpur, Guru Nanak sees the agony of the people whom the Moghul hath "conquered" and who are crying, weeping and wailing, "O Lord!" asks Guru Nanak, in agony of his heart, "hast Thou not felt? The hounds, alas! have ruined the jewels,—innocent lives,—and none heedeth the dead. Towns cities and palaces have perished: and princes have been cut up and rolled in dust. Mughals and Pathans have fought and matched their swords on the field of battle." Guru Nanak felt the vastness of the agony of India. "Kings," he said, "are butchers, and cruelty is their knife: the world is suffering endless pain: how shall it be saved?"

Forces of nihilism were growing. Islam, forgetful of her mystics and saints, was entangled in the externals of *shariat*. To the majority of the Hindus, Islam was no better than a religion of the

Sword. In Kasi, in Jagannath, in Hardwar, he saw that Hinduism was no better than a religion of rites and ceremonies. And there were many to whom rites and ceremonies were meaningless, many who, in their hearts, denied or doubted the Eternal. It was a period of externalism, materialism and nihilistic rebelliousness against the Spirit. Like a beacon, blazing out into darkness, shone Nanak, his light of love gradually overpowering the nihilism of that dark age in history.

To all he gave the love of his heart. This love converted the notorious robber, Shaikh Sajjan. Under Nanak's spell, Shaikh Sajjan distributed, among the poor, his stolen wealth, and became a disciple of the great Prophet of Love. The magnetism of his love in fluenced the Islamic countries he visited, as he travelled in the blue garb of a Muslim pilgrim. In love he spoke to the *mullahs* of Mecca and his words went into their hearts:—

How great is God!
The greatest of the great is He.
And great is His Word!
Men are specks:
Yet, alas! they depart this life in pride!

Nanak's love rivetted to him the faithful Mardana, who accompanied the Master in his many travels to Afghanistan and Ceylon, to Mecca and Medina, to Baghdad and Multan. Nanak's love flowed out to Lehna, and this worshipper of Durga became "Angad,"—a limb of the Master's body, an integral part of Nanak's radiant soul!

Nanak And Luther

I have heard a number of Sikhs refer to Guru Nanak as the "Luther" of India. Guru Nanak and Luther, I humbly submit, belong to two different classes. Luther was a "Reformer," Nanak was a Saint. Luther's picture is that of a man of stubborn individuality:

gazing at the picture of Guru Nanak, I am impressed with his humility. Luther's "Letters' and his "Table-Talk" (in 6 volumes) reveal his "ego-complex" in his assaults upon his "enemies." The great Guru had no "enemies:" he blessed those that jailed him: he gave his love to all who persecuted him.

A flame was in the heart of each: Luther's "flame" aroused Germany to "protest" against the Roman Catholic Church. Nanak's "flame" kindled in many hearts the love of God and Man. Luther was a dynamic personality: the Pope asked his chamberlain to bring Luther from Wittenberg to Rome, but the chamberlain returned and reported that even an army of 25 thousands would be insufficient to get Luther out of the country. When Nanak was arrested by Babur's men and asked to go to jail, Nanak walked humbly to his prison-cell, saying:—"Thy will be done, O Ordainer who ordereth as it pleaseth Thee!"

Luther was a Voice of Revolt: Nanak was a Prophet of Renaissance. Luther opposed the poor peasants who, being oppressed, rose in rebellion and demanded their human rights: Luther asked the rulers to put down the "Peasants' Revolt" with a heavy hand by killing the peasants as "mad dogs," and he wrote a virulent pamphlet "Against the Thievish, Murderous Hordes of Peasants." Nanak was a lover of the peasants and a servant of the poor.

Not of Luther, but of Buddha am I reminded as I think of Nanak, the gentle Apostle of the poor, the Prophet of Love to all. Read his sermon in the mosque at Sultanpur: what a vision he has to the spirit of religion! He denounces no religion: he proclaims that Religion is life, not theology, is Deed not creed.

"Caste and birth," he says, "are of no avail!
"Ask those who know the Truth.
"Caste and Birth are defined by deeds!
"And look at the Light within!"

Alone With God

Nanak is a psychic. Suddenly, one morning, after his bath, he has a vision in the *tapoban*, the Forest of meditation, situated on the other side of the river Ravi. This "vision" thrills Nanak: a Voice speaks to him:—"Nanak! I am with thee! Repeat My Name: and ask others to repeat My Name. Mingle with men, uncontaminated by the world! Worship, meditate, and serve the poor!"

It is the first "ecstasy" of Nanak. It filled him and out of the fullness of his heart, he sings:—

> O Lord!
> If I had hundreds of thousands of tons of paper,
> And if my ink were inexhaustible,
> And if my pen moved swift as the rushing wind,
> I should still be unable
> To articulate all Thou art!

Nanak has a vision of the "Infinite." This vision fills him: and, three days later, as he returns from the woods and re-appears at his residence, he prepares, in obedience to the vision, to go forth among the people to sing to them the Name of God,—the *Sat-Nama*,—and to ask them all to sing the Name Divine. And, before he moves out on his travels, he gives away absolutely all his possessions to the poor. Jesus asked the rich, young ruler to give all he had to the poor, if he would walk in the way of the Lord: and the young man failed at the test. Guru Nanak obeys the call of his "vision" to the letter, and goes out, empty-handed, to give God's great message to the people. "Nanak knoweth none other than God,"—says this humble apostle of the Infinite. And again:—"I only know one God: His way would I indicate unto men."

Western writers say Nanak resembled Paul in the extent of his travels. Nanak travelled much more widely than Paul. Nanak's life was that of a pilgrimage to the Infinite. He preached to the king and queen of Ceylon. He spoke of his Lord to the *yogis* in the Himalayan *ashramas*. He gave a message on "God,—the Universal Spirit" in front of the Kaaba in Mecca. When the Arab priest said to Nanak, "Why hast thou O sinner, turned thy feet towards the Kaaba,—the seat of God?" Nanak' in deep humility, said:— "Brother! turn my feet in the direction in which God is not!"

Nurshah placed her silver and gold, her jewels and coral at Nanak's feet but could not tempt him. "The only Treasure," he said, "is the Name of God!" And Nurshah and her women associate became Nanak's disciples. He blessed a group of robbers and they gave to the poor all they had and turned farmers.

To a group of Muslims, he said:—

> He is a Muslim who is patient and pure
> And free from the taint of self.

And as they listened to the words, they exclaimed:—"Allah is speaking in Nanak!"

Nanak too, said:—"There is no Hindu and no Muslim." "Hindu" and "Muslim" are our names for masks: behind the masks is "Man." Nanak realised the unity of Hindus and Muslims in the Man Universal. Nanak's was the Religion of Man. The emphasis, in his message, was not on s criptures and ceremonials, but on life,—on love of God and right action. In a beautiful song, Nanak sings:—

> I have turned my heart into a boat:
> I have searched in every sea:
> I have dwelt by rivers and streams:
> I have bathed at places of pilgrimage:
> I have lived in forests and glades:
> I have eaten bitter and sweet:
> I have seen remotest regions:
> Yea: I have beheld heavens upon heavens:
> And this have I learnt
> That he is true to his faith
> Who loveth God and Man
> And, serving all, abideth in the Good!

A vision of the Infinite filled his heart. Who hath known Him? Who can comprehend Him? And in His Presence who can say that he is pure? "Why callest thou me good? There is none good but one,"—said Jesus. And Nanak said:—"My sins are numerous as the waters of the sea and the waves of the ocean." Nanak called himself "weak," "foolish" and "ignorant." "How can I show my face?" he said. Nanak's "God-consciousness" was that of the "Infinite" in whose Presence Nanak realised that "ego" was an illusion, that he was "nought," a zero!

A Creative Mind

The life and teaching of Guru Nanak megnetised many homes in the Punjab and in Sind. In the North and North-West of India arose Orders paying homage to Nanak and calling themselves "Nanak-Shahis." They studied philosophy and practised a purely religious life in the light of Guru Nanak's teaching. Some years ago, they published two big Sanskrit volumes on Philosophy ascribed to Nanak, and named "The Nirakara Mimansa" and the "Adhbhuta Gita."

These books will not be appreciated by the "secularists" of modern India who, indeed, have gone a step beyond even Voltaire, the French free-thinker, who wrote, as a last confession, the words:—"I die in adoration of God!" The "secularists" think that faith in God is a dogma of the "dark middle ages" and they feel proud of "modern enlightenment," which regards religion as an "opiate" for the people and *Puja* or "worship" as merely a symptom of "functional disorders in the brain." The "secularists" bow to "nature" and "reason" as their "gods" and to "neo-materialism" as the last word in the philosophy of life! Guru Nanak was a creative mind, and he bore witness to God and Truth (*Sat Nama*) and Brotherhood of all Faiths and all Peoples. Guru Nanak submitted not to dictatorship of secularism.

The teaching of Guru nanak is supported by the witness of the creative minds of the era in which we live,—the witness of poets and artists, of thinkers and scientists. Beethoven wrote in his "Diary" the words which thrill me:—"You alone can inspire me,—You, my God, my salvation, my rock, my all! In you alone will I put my trust!" Paul Claudel emphasised the thought that poetry bore witness to God! To him poetry and prayers were two expressions of one simple urge of the human soul. And Strindberg closed his life on the following significant note:—"I am through with life, and the balance shows that the Word of God is alone right!" "In the universe," wrote A.N. Whitehead, the eminent teacher of Applied Mathematics, "there is a Unity. We call this Unity, God!"

In his "Hymn of Creation,"—the *Arati* Song,—the Guru sings of that Deeper Religion in which Faith and Science meet each other reconciled, harmonised, unified in the One Spirit. The Guru says:—

The sun and the moon
Are the lamps lighted in the Heaven
Which is Thy salver: and the Lights
Move round and round Thee,—Beloved!

*

From Thy radiance is raMdiant everything:
By the Light of Thy Face
The stars burn bright: Thou art
The Soul, the Life, the Light of all,—Beloved!

•

Give Thou, O Lord! the water of Thy grace
To the little bird,—this heart,—that thirsts for Thee:
O come and bend on me Thy beauteous Face!
So may Nanak in Thy Name abide,—Beloved!

The saints of God are like temple-bells. Each has a note of the Music of Eternity. Nanak's is a note of unity. Nanak sings in the "Guru Granth":—

The One is in eye, in word, in mouth:
The One is in all the worlds.
In sleeping is the One:
In walking is the One:
In the One be thou absorbed!
In all the One abides!
The universe rests in the One!
O Thou, the Fulness of Joy,

Bestow Thy Mercy on me!
I recognise all as Thee!
One is He,
And He Himself is many!
Nanak says:—He, the One, every abides in all!

One recalls the words of Jami, the Persian poet:—

Blend into One every soul
And every form and every place:
See the One!
Know the One!
Speak of the One!
Aspire to the One!
Seek the One!
And ever chant of the One!

In this night of civilisation, let India meditate on the Guru's great message of the One: and in his pure, sacrificial life and song, let India find a new alphabet of that true Freedom which reflects the Lotus-face of the inner Light but which, alas! our Caesars do not see!

Kabir And Nanak

Nanak's love and humility inspired his disciples with boundless affection. They spread his message, far and wide, in the North: they purified the life of the Punjab: they build a New Brotherhood of the Strong, and they gave a new hope, a new faith, a new life to the Hindus of Muslim Sind. Nanak became the beloved of the Hindus in that province. Scattered, today, in different parts of India,—homeless exiles,—they still are attached to the name and person of Nanak: they still love him with a love, as pure as it is profound. Nanak infused a new spirit in the North and in Sind. South India knows him not: and the Western world knows him not. The West, broken and bleeding, needs, as never before, the message of Nanak's life and Nanak's gospel of love. Who will take the message to the nations of the world?

Nanak saw the world's deep tragedy: he saw the world caught in a net of suffering and woe: he saw the agony of the earth,—its travail and pain: he saw the anguish of India, oppressed by dark forces, trampled upon by conflicts of creeds and dark deeds. And he prayed for God's grace to "save the world in agony." "Raise all unto Thee," he cried, "raise them whichever way they may be raised!" And he taught that "the *Nama*, the *Sat Nama*, the Word of God" was the cure of all the ills of "suffering humanity." The "Word of God," the "*Sat Nama*" singeth in the heart of him who strives to be pure. "Be pure," said the Guru, "that Truth may be realised."

The pure spirit of Religion was incarnated in this apostle of humility and love. Year after year hath he come nearer to me, and he hath enkindled in my heart a love, which adores him as one of the world's truly great ones, who attained to surpassing greatness, because they were "great" as they were "pure." Nanak breathes on his *bhaktas* a breath, a benediction of the Eternal. Nanak thrills us with his "naturalness": Nanak needs no legends of a superhuman world: the beauty of his simple, humble life lures us on to his vision of the Infinite. No miraculous legends need embellish his life. He is so natural, so human: therefore, he shines with a beauty divine!

It was a priviledge epoch in which India could produce two such inspired and illuminated geniuses as Nanak and Kabir. It was a divine hour in India's history. How many hidden forces came to a head in Nanak as Kabir! Nanak was a farmer: Kabir was a weaver. Each was so simple, so humble. Each adored the one Eternal God in all. "There is no Hindu and there is no Muslim," said Nanak. Kabir called himself "a child of Ram and Allah." Each sang the one Divine Name. "O God!" said Kabir, whether Allah or Rama, I live by Thy Name!" Each asked his countrymen to turn away from the outer religion of rites and ceremonies to the inner religion of the heart.

Guru Nanak preached a Faith which adored the one God,—the *Karta Purukh*, the Supreme Person who is the Creator of all: Guru Nanak pointed out that purification was from within, not in temple-rites and pilgrimage to holy places: and Guru Nanak adored the one God whom idols and the images of God could not reach. "Lifeless," said Kabir, "are all the images of the Gods: they cannot speak: I know it, for I have called aloud to them." And again:— "What avails it to wash your mouth and count your beads and bathe in holy streams and bow in temples, if deceitfulness is in your hearts?"

Nanak, like Kabir, had no dogmas: each bore witness to the One Name and purity in thought and word and deed and service of the poor. Nanak spoke of God as the One beyond conception and speech,—the Formless One,—in whose presence the mind is still, the tongue is speechless, the heart is dumb. And Kabir sang:—

> There be a world beyond all bounds,
> Brother! And there is a Being
> Whom no name may name aright,
> Of whom the best we cay say
> Is that nothing can be said:
> No form, no body, no length, no breadth
> Hath He: He *is*. But how can I describe it?
> The words of the mouth tell of It,—nought!
> The letters on paper,—write of It,—nought!

Both Nanak and Kabir asked the seeker to look for the Light within. "Wanderers are they," says Nanak, "who seek Him abroad." And Kabir says:—

> The Real is in your home within!
> Why wander you from forest to forest?
> Go where you will, to Kasi or to Mathura,
> You will not find Him
> Except in your soul within!

Both Kabir and Nanak were mystics of the purest ray serene. Both were prophets of the "Inner Life," and both urged that the "Inner" should be expressed, not in creeds, dogmas, rites and ceremonies, but in humble service of the poor and lowly. And service of the poor must be inspired by love of God and of *Nama*,—

the Word of God. Nanak sings:—

O man! how canst thou be Free without Love?
And the Word of God,—the *Nama*,—
Will reveal to thee the Lord within thee,
And grant thee treasures of love.
O man! love Him as lotus loves the water:
The more it is beaten by the waves, the more doth
it unfold itself:
In water is the life of the lotus:
And without water the lotus dies.
O man! love God as the fish loveth water:
The more the water, the more joyous is the fish:
Without water, the fish liveth not for a moment,
God knoweth its heartache!
May I be a fish and, living in water, know the
secret of life!
O man! love God as the *chatrik* loveth rain!
The tanks may be full
And the land may be green.
But the *chatrik* is not happy
Without a drop of rain from above.
O man! love God as the *chakur* love the sun:
The *chakur* sleepeth not for a moment
Without the sun:
The *chakur* liveth close to what is so far away!

Love-filled, the seeker becometh a bride of the Lord. Nanak says:—

Let the disciple become
The Bridegroom's bride!
Filled with *bhakti*,
Let the disciple be dyed
In the true colour of Love.
Such a bride shall never be a widow:
For she abideth in the Sat Guru:
On her forehead is the jewel of Love:
And without the Bridegroom

She knoweth none.
Awake! Awake! O seeker, awake!
Behold! Thy Bridegroom is awake!
Renounce the little wisdom of thy "ego":
Love-filled, think ever of His Lotus-Feet!
Do as He biddeth thee to do:
Surrender thy body and thy soul to Him:
Surrender thyself:
So mayst thou meet thy Lord.
The day He looks on thee
Shall count as the blessed day,
And thou shalt all the treasures gain:
Loved by the Lord,
Thou shalt rejoice as the wedded one:
Thou shalt be a Queen!
Living day and night in love.
Thou shalt be perfect
in beauty, wisdom, love!
May I be, ever and always, the *suhagan*
(wedded bride)
Absorbed in Him for ever!
And garlands of flowers shall I put on.
And decorations shall I wear,
When my Beloved,—the Bridegroom,—
Shall come unto me!

Absorbed in the Lord of Love, in disciple will grow in meditation of the Word of God. This meditation is *jap*,—the *mantra*,—which involves the eight-fold exercise or *sadhana*:—(1) purity of body and mind; (2) silence; (3) concentration of mind; (4) realisation of the meaning of the *mantra*; (5) patience and contentment; (6) faith and reverence; (7) *sat-sang* which is *sant-sang*, fellowship with pure and holy ones; (8) *living* the *mantra* in daily life. "May I be a kokil-bird," says the Guru, "living in the mango-grove and singing the notes of meditation: so may I meet my Master!"

Without this "meditation," *tapasya* and good deeds are fruitless. Such deeds do but lead the seeker astray from the Path. The seeker, whose mind and heart meditate on the Word of God, is a

Gurmukh: but he, whose mind and heart wander away from the Lord, is a *manmukh*: he may do many benevolent deeds, but him the Guru calls a *sakat*: he is a "smoked vessel": his company "soils," gives a "stain" to the seeker.

In both, Kabir and Nanak, the Spirit of History kindled a celestial fire. Both bore witness to an Eternity that dwells in the heart within,—an Eternity, a Divinity, that is the destiny of every man,—if he will but develop his heroic will, renouncing the littleness of self-love or the "ego."

Kabir and Nanak,—both sang of love. Kabir found his interpreter to the West in Tagore: Nanak awaits his interpreters,—apostles of humility and love: they will thrill the world with the story of a man who renounced the joys of this world to live alone for his Father,—the *Akal Purukha*,—the Father of all creation. The tale of Guru Nanak, re-told in simple terms as that of a man amongst men, of one who was and still is our Brother, our Elder Brother, a Leader of our pilgrim-band to the Eternal Shrine,—will move multitudes in East and West to tears that will purify the nations. And his message, re-interpreted in terms of modern consciousness, will awaken in the best minds and hearts of Asia and of the West a vision of the Infinite that will bring together both science and religion in worship of the One Mystery that no man may know,—the One Life that breathes its benediction on the pathways of Nature and procession of history through the ages.

Nanak was a creator of an epoch in India history. Other creators yet may come in the unfoldings of time. But Nanak's humility will not, I believe, be surpassed. And when India comes back to her own and is truly a Free State,—not an imitation "secular state,"—the sons and daughters of the motherland will renew their youth in reverence for Nanak as one of the noblest of inspired geniuses in the history of Man.

Secrets Of The Self

Guru Nanak travelled, far and wide: he preached the Gospel of the God-life, wherever he went.

In his Four Rounds, Guru Nanak covered India, Tibet, Ceylon and Eastern countries dominated by Islam. These Four Rounds are called Four "*yatras*," "pilgrimages" of Guru Nanak.

In the First Round, he visited Kurukshetra, Karnal, Panipat, Hardwar, Delhi, Brindaban, Gorakhmatha, Ayodhya, Luchnow, Banaras, Patna, Gaya, Dacca, Assam, Chittagong and Jagannath Puri. He returned through the Vindhya Mountain, Central India and Rajputana.

In the Second Round, he visited Bikaneer, Ajmere, Pushkar, Abu, Ujjain, Madras, Nagapatam, and Lanka. On his return, he visited Rameshwaram, Dwarka, Kathiawar, Sind, Satghara, Talwandi and Lahore.

In Colombo, Guru Nanak sang a song in answer to the query of the king of Lanka, Raja Shiv Nabh:—"Do you follow the practices of *yogis* or *sanyasins* or monks of some other order?" Mardana played the tune, and the Guru sang:—

> When Thou callest me within.
> I commune with Thee, O Lord!
> In Thy Pure Name is my *yoga*:
> In love of Thee is the end of death
> And the end of life:
> Who liveth in Thy Word,—the Revelation of Thy
> Spirit,—
> He rises above all doubt,
> And remaineth, day and night,
> In Thy service!

The Raja listened to the song and wept. *Pran Sangli*,—of which only a fragment remains,—was, also, sung by the Guru in Ceylon.

In Lahore, the Guru met Duni Chand, a wealthy *khatri*. The Guru gave Duni Chand a needle and said:—"Duni Chand, keep it with thee, and give it back to me in the next world!" And Duni Chand said:—"Master! this needle I cannot carry after death: how can I return it?" "What use then, Duni Chand, are thy millions to thee?" And Duni Chand was changed: he spent much of what he had in the service of the poor, and became a devoted disciple of the Guru.

In the Third Round, he set out for the Himalayan Mountains and visited the Mansarowar Lake, where he had discourses with the *yogis.* He visited Garwal, Hemakuta, Gorakhpur, Sikkim, Bhutan and Tibet. It is believed that the Guru, also, visited China. He returned through the Kailas Mountains and through Ladakh, Kashmir, Riasi and Jammu. In the Cave Temples in the Mansarowar Lake, you may still see images of Guru Nanak: and there are hill-tribes there who worship Guru Nanak, calling him "Bhadra Guru," the Great Master."

In the Fourth Round, he travelled to Sind (a second time), Dwarka in Kathiawar, and Mecca and Medina in Arabia. He, also, visited Baghdad. He travelled, also, to Jerusalem, Damascus and Alleppo. We are told he, also, visited Stambul (Constantinople). Some would have us believe that he, also, visited Egypt or Sudan. In Mecca, he made the startling statements:—"Is there a place where the House of God is not?" "Narrow is the path through which a man must pass who would reach the shrine where shineth the Glory of God." He returned from Baghdad to Bharata through Baku, Persia, Turkestan, kabul and Peshawar. A Gurudwara still stands in Kabul and is associated with the name of Guru Nanak.

Everywhere he held *sat-sang* and gave the message of *Sat-Nama*.

For twenty-five years and more, the great Teacher travelled, from place to place, preaching and singing the Name of the One God of all nations, of all religions and races.

Then he came back to Kartarpur and stayed there, cultivating his farm, holding *sat-sang*, every morn and every night, and mingling with the poor, simple folk, who travelled to him from neighbouring villages.

His well-known "Songs" and "Sayings" have been collected in these five scriptures:—(1) Japji; (2) Patti; (3) Arati; (4) Dakshiṅiya Omkar; and (5) Sinhagoshti.

"Who is a saint?"—they ask him: and he says:—

He who forgetteth not the Beloved
In a single breath of his being:
He who treasures the Name
In his inner consciousness:
Blessed, indeed, is he:
Such an one is a Perfect Saint!

In another passage, Nanak says:—

The true saint of God
Knows Him nigh, all the hours of day and night!
And sweet to him is the will of God
And all that the Lord ordains!
The One Name is the Support of his life.
His joy is in singing the Name.
In friend and foe he beholds
The Light of the only One!
He knoweth nought but God!
With folded hands I pray:—
"O Lord! grant me
The service of such a saint!"

The true saint of God, Guru Nanak teaches, is a man who (1) looks within, (2) is humble, (3) is a servant of the poor, and (4) adores the Eternal One. Nanak says:—

He dwells within in all his work:
He wanders not abroad!
He drinks the nectar in his heart:
Why need he wander after poison?
He meditates on the Name:
He is a servant of all!
"Call thou me not good," he says:
And none he calleth evil!

Again:—

I am a sinner:

Thou alone art pure!
As full as is the sea
Of water and its drops,
So full am I of sins.
Thy mercy I crave!
Have compassion, Lord!
My life is as a sinking stone:
How can it cross the sea
Without Thy grace?
A sinner am I:
Thou art the True, the Infinite:
Forgive the sinner, Lord!

*

The Name is the King above all Kings:
The Name alone can carry me across!

*

Beautiful and fair, beyond compare,
Is the palace of my Lord!
Adorned with gems, with pearls and gold
Is the palace of the Purest One:
His castle is enchanting!
Without a ladder how may I ascend?
The Guru is the Ladder.
Without a boat there is no road on the sea:
The Guru is the Boat!

*

Who is the Guru? The word is derived from the root *gri*, to "utter." The Guru is he who "utters," who "vibrates" the "Name." The Guru, also, means one who is the "Light in darkness." The Guru is illumination in the "darkness" of this world: and the Guru vibrates with the "*Nama*," the "Name": the Guru, with his vibration of the "Word," purifies, illuminates, and leads the disciple through darkness into the Light,—leads him on to "union" with the Lord.

Nanak says:—

Without the Guru, there is darkness:
Without the *Nama*, the Name, the Word, there is
 no understanding.
If I abide within the Name,
The Name doth come and dwell within my heart!
The Guru utters the Word, the Name,
And death dwells not where the Word abides!

And "death" is forgetfulness: he who forgets the Lord is really "dead." Guru Nanak's message to multitudes was:—"Awake! Awake!"

Nanak says:—

My Beloved is awake, ever awake!
Alas! I have fallen asleep!

The awakened soul is, by the grace of the Guru, led on the union with the Lord. And the mark of him, who is with the Lord united, is love. Listen to what Nanak says:—

The soul, who by the true Guru is united to the Lord,
Abideth in *bhakti*, in devotion supreme.
Love, O Nanak! is her companion!

He who dwelleth in devotion, *bhakti*,—he hath overcome death. Love is life. Guru Nanak's call to every true seeker after God is:—"Die before you are physically dead!" "Be dead," he says, "in this body before you depart at death." Be dead to the world before you die! Nanak says:—

He that dies by the Word of the Guru,
He will not die again!

To live in Love is to be united with God. Be united in Him, and do your daily task in this world, which is, indeed, a "play" of the Lord: "the play," says Nanak, "lasts today and tomorrow": the "play" is a "passing show": but beyond is the "Beloved": beyond is the "*Sat loka*," the Realm of the One Divine Reality, where abide the Saints, the Pure Ones, who live in joy and in service of the Lord! So let him who would seek the Perfect Life,—the life of Love,—

purify himself and aspire to adore the one Lord in all. "Duality," says Nanak, "sinks the boat's load." Let the seeker realise that God is all in all! Let the seeker breathe out, by day and by night, awake and asleep, in the daily work of life, in his thoughts and in every movement of his heart, the one aspiration:—"Thou alone! Thou alone!" "Tera!" "Tera!" "Thine!" "Thine am I!" "Thine alone!"

I recall what the mystic poet, Hafiz, says in the song of adoring ecstasy:—

> On the tablet of the universe is no letter save Thy Name:
> By which Name, then, shall we invoke Thee?

"*Tera*!" "*Tera*!" "*Thine*!" "Thine alone!"

So doth Nanak adore the One, again and again. Infinite is the One: adorable but indescribable. "How can I describe Thee?" Nanak asks. No human tongue, no hymn of man, no song of a sage or saint, may describe Him who transcendeth speech and mind. As the Persian mystic, Nizami, says:—"He clips the tongue of all who adore the Secret, lest they repeat the Secret of the King."

Guru Nanak points out that man suffers because he has entangled himself in the "ego," the little "self." The ego is the cause of suffering and sin. Love of the "self" is the cause of pain: the cure of pain is to renounce "self" and escape unto the Word, the *Nama*, the Name,—unto God. The little "self" is a "dark shadow" of unreality. To escape from it, be non-egoistic, be humble, annihilate the *aham* the "I,"—and, looking inward and upward and all around to the One, see the Light,—nothing but the Light. And he beholds the Light, Guru Nanak teaches, who has *bhakti*, love.

Such a man has attained to what no tongue may tell. He is speechless: he but exclaims:—"*Tera !*" "*Tera !*" He hath gained the Inexpressible: and from him "no news returns." He hath grown to the God-life by process of dying. He hath gradually died from the man and grown the wings of the angels: and from the angels, too, he hath advanced, until he hath attained the *Sat-loka*,—the Realm of the Eternal,—where God shines, God and His *bhaktas* and His saints, the seers of the One Face Divine, the seers of the "Hidden Treasure," the "Hidden Mystery," that is the "Seer" beyond all seers, the vision of all *bhaktas* and saints. Guru Nanak refers to this "Hidden Mystery," again and again, as the "Beloved," in whose Love the heart hath life. In this "Hidden Mystery" be hid for ever: and so learn to love and suffer silently: be hid, be as "nought."

In his songs, Guru Nanak sounds this note, again and again:—renounce self-seeking: adore the "Hidden Mystery" with love in thy heart, and seek nor name nor fame, nor sign nor tale for future time. This love, nonegoistic love, alone will loose thee from thyself. Do thy daily work, but entangle not thyself in any form, in any finite thing: for this world is but a bridge. Linger not on the bridge, but move on to the Shrine, O Pilgrim of *Satyaloka*! Do thy daily work, but escape from thyself. Do thy daily work, but in each act think of the One, meditate on the "King," the "Father," the "Friend," the Eternally Beautiful, the "Beloved."

Bahlol,—The Blessed

Baghdad was, in Nanak's days, a centre of Muslim culture: Baghdad, too, was a homeland of *pirs* and *sufi fakirs*. Guru Nanak stayed in Baghdad for four months and had talks with some of the holy men of that place. One of them was named Bahlol. Nanak sang of the Infinity of God and His inifinite creation. Bahlol said the *Koran* had mentioned seven earths and seven heavens only. Guru Nanak urged that the universe was not confined to seven earths and seven heavens but had millions and millions of planets and worlds: and the Guru greeted all in the name of *Sat Kartar*. The Guru disarmed all opposition, and Bahlol and his son were convinced of the truth of the Guru's teaching. Bahlol and his son became *bhaktas* of Guru Nanak and joined Him in adoring God as the Infinite.

Sri Ananda Acharya was an Indian *swami*, who travelled to many part of the world: one of them was Baghdad. He wrote a book, in English, named, "Snow Birds." It is a record of his travels. He settled in Norway,—I am told. This is what he wrote in his

"Snow Birds":—

"(On reading an Arabic inscription in a shrine outside the town of Baghdad).

"Upon this slab of granite didst thou sit discoursing of love and holy light, O Guru Nanak! Prince among India's holy ones!

"What songs didst thou sing to charm the soul of Iran!

"What peace from Himalaya's lonely caves and forests didst thou carry to the groves and rose-gardens of Baghdad!

What light from Badrinath's snowy peak didst thou bear to illuminate the heart of Bahlol,—they saintly Iranian disciple!

"Eight fortnights did Bahlol hearken to thy words on Life and its Mystery, on the Path and the Spring Eternal, while the moon waxed and waned in the pomegranate groves beside the grass-covered Desert of the Dead!

"And after thou, O Nanak, didst depart for thy beloved Bharat, Bahlol, the *fakir*, spoke to none: he listened not to the voice of man. And his fame spread, far and wide, and the Shah of Iran came to pay him homage: but the holy *fakir* took no earthly treasure nor listened to the praise of kings and courtiers.

"Thus lived he,—lonely, devoted thoughtful for sixty years, sitting before the stone on which thy sacred feet had rested.

"And ere he left this house of *avidya*, he wrote these words on the stone:—

"'Here spake the Hindu Guru Nanak to *fakir* Bahlol, and for these sixty years, since the Guru left Iran, the soul of Bahlol has rested on the Master's Word,—like a bee poised on a dawnlit honey rose.'"

This place is known to the Arabs of Baghdad as the tomb of Bahlol: and in the centre is a picture of Sri Guru Nanak. On this memorial is an inscription in the Turkish language: and the words are, in English translation, these:—

"Murad saw the demolished building of Hazrat Rab-i-majid, Baba Nanak, Faki Aulia; and Murad re-built it with his own hands, so that the historic memorial may continue, from generation to generation, and that Baba Nanak's *murid-i-s'eed* (the blessed disciple) may obtain heavenly bliss."

From Baghdad Guru Nanak returned to the Punjab, after passing through Baku, Persia, Turkestan, Kabul and Peshawar. With the mighty power of love he blessed all he met and all he saw,—flowers and trees and birds and beasts, sunrise and sunset on the hills. Love he gave to all,—love to all creation, to men and women and children of all creeds, of all countries and, as he sang his songs of love, the song of birds blended their notes with his adoration of the one Infinite Mystery. With love in his heart, Nanak returned to Bharata,—returned to his mission among the sons and daughters of the motherland.

The Song Of Nanak

Nanak was a singer of the Infinite. He poured the Infinite within him into his songs to the people: the very river sang his songs: the stars burnt, as little lamps, as the heart within him sang *arati* to the Infinite.

Music greeted him, we read, as he was born in the dawn of a moon-lit night, in spring: and music flowed out of him,—his life and his lips,—as he travelled, from place to place, on his mission. Nanak's *Japji*,—the Gita of the Sikhs,—is melodious with the music of the flute. The music of the *Kirtan Sohila* enchants us with a song, which floats to us from a far-off Realm of Beauty and Blessedness,—the Realm of Grace (*Fazal*),—which is the highest hope for man.

The Infinite sings in all the five scriptures, which enshrine the Guru's *bani*,—the *Pancharatnas*,—of Guru Nanak. Listen to the words in the *Japji*:—

This Earth, they say, is borne
On horns of the Bull.
Not the Bull, but *Dharma*,—the Law,—
Bears the weight of the world.
But this Earth is not the only one:
There is Earth beyond this earth,
And there are planets beyond,
And planets still beyond!

Who can comprehend the Infinite? Unknowable is the One,—illimitable, inexhaustible, immeasurable, inexpressible! At His Throne "wait a million prophets," and "in the interval of His one eye-wink, there are a million creations that come and go."

Yet this Infinite is the "Beloved" and Nanak is never tired of singing songs to the Beloved: Nanak is lost in the perpetual music of His praise. Nanak sings:—

The fish knows not the nature of the sea,
Knows not how wide, how vast
And how deep the ocean is:
So I know Thee not, O Infinite!
But Thou art my Beloved,
And I touch Thee,
I live in Thee,
And I shall die,
If Thou wilt take me out of Thee!

Again:—

The arrow of His gracious glance
Hath wounded me!
In the Temple within I sit:
It is the Temple of Love:
My Body is a robe divine:
The sacred nectar floweth
In the Temple within:
The *Nama*,—the Word that revealeth the Spirit,—
Is the breath of my breath,
And Song is the blood of my being!

*

O Beloved! think of me!
O everywhere, in every throb of life
Thou art! All temples of flesh
Are Thine: the Teacher and Inspirer
Art Thou of all:
I know no other but Thee!
I sing of Thee as Thou singest in me:
Beloved! Thy throne is Eternity,
And Thy Name is mighty,
And Thy Glory hath no end!

*

Truth art Thou! And Justice Thou!
The Temple Art Thou,
And the Lord of the Temple Thou!
And in Thy Temple Thou dost sing
To Thee and worship Thee!

*

The Beloved asks thee to put off
All vestures of vanity,
Or the Beloved will not come home!
The Beloved loves the vestures
Dyed in *Nama*, dyed in the dye of Love:
And the brides who wear
The vestures dyed in this colour, rich and pure,
Abide in Him,
And He cometh to dwell in them,
I pray for the dust of the feet
Of such blessed brides!
Them, He doth decorate:
Them, He doth dye with the colour of the soul,—
With Himself!
And they no longer roam abroad,
They wander not,
Seeking Him outside:

For in the heart within
Have they found their King:
The Heart becometh His Throne!

*

There, there, in thine own Heart
He waits for thee,—thy King!
And the way to Him
Is the way of Love.
Love Him,—love not thyself!
Think as He thinketh!
Will as He willeth!
Do as He biddest!
Forego thyself,
And think of His Lotus Feet alone!
And find thy home in Him!
Nothing else thou needest!
At His Lotus Feet find
Beauty, wisdom, love!

*

I seek not pleasure,—
For pleasure makes me sick:
I know that pain is a healer:
I do but ask of Thee
That I may not forget Thee!
Thou hast made me
And Thou dost know!
So what Thou doest
Blesseth me!
And what I do
Becomes my undoing!

*

Infinite art Thou!
Yet in Thy mercy Thou dost dwell
In what Thou hast made,
And Thou hast no limit, O Limitless One!

Further than the furthest art Thou,
And still further, O Infinite One!

*

Creation is Thy magic, Thy miracle:
And Thou, Magician, dost dwell therein!
All life doth burn in Thee,
And Thou dost burn in the flame of life!

*

Palaces of pearls and rubies are nought,
And walls and floors with musk
And sandal plastered are nought!
Turn not thine eyes from the vision of the One,—
Real is He,—He alone!
And forget not His Name,—my "Beloved"!

*

O jewel of my heart!
Who can value Thee?
And to whom may I go,
Who may teach me Thy worth?
If Thou are mine, all is mine!
For Thou art the Self
Of all the world, of all creation!
Who can set a price on Thee?
Thou art Thine own Price!
Thou art the Seer of Thyself!

O jewel of my heart!
If I touch Thee, I live:
And touching Thee again
I live yet more!

In love is the secret of spiritual life. And to love is to sacrifice all you are to the Lord. "I shall sever my head off," says the Guru, "and offer it to the Lord, and I shall then serve Him without a head on my body. Why shall I not die? Why shall I not give up my life to the Lord? Why shall I not glorify the Lord in dying for Him? Wouldst thou tread the Path? Come with thy head on the palm of thy hand! Sacrifice thy head! Waver not!"

Guru Nanak dedicated his life to the service of Love. And Love took him by the hand and led him on, from place to place, to preach, to teach, to bear witness to Divine Light, to unearthly inspiration. Guru Nanak was possessed by the dynamic power of Love: he was Love-possessed, God-possessed. And in far-off countries, as in the land of his birth, he revealed to prince and peasant, to Hindu and Muslim, the shining truth of Indwelling Love. And Love has but one movement. It knows no difference of time or place or person. As the sparks always fly upwards, so Love, rejoicing in itself and seeking no reward, ever ascends upwards, blessing all and being blessed by the One Spirit. To love God is to live in the purity of love and to rise out of the power of evil into the freedom of the Sons of God.

Amid The Lowly And The Lost

Nanak's life at Sultanpur is a chant to God, and an incense unto the poor. He is in charge of the "Stores": he sells flour and rice and ghee and oil to the customers. Some of them are too poor to pay: he pays for them: he hath opened his heart and opened his hands in service of the destitute and the disinherited, the lowly and the lost. As the violets dream of spring, so doth his heart dream of a Tomorrow when the poor shall come to their own.

Nanak is a lover of the simple and the poor. At Amenabad, he knocks at the door of a carpenter's house: Nanak wishes to stay for a few days in the cottage of Lalo. Lalo takes a little time to open the door. "Lalo!" the Guru asks, "why so late?" And Lalo, bowing to the Guru, says:—"Master! I was busy." "Doing what?" asks the Guru, and Lalo says:—"Master! I was mending wooden pegs for the walls." "Mending wooden pegs?" the Master asks: and the question goes home into the heart of Lalo. Surely, life is meant for something better than mending wooden pegs! And Lalo's life is changed. Says Nanak:—

Thou art here, O man!
To gain the Real!
Alas! thou art engaged in trash:
And behold!
The night is about to end!

In Rohelkhand, the Rohela clan of the Afghans had settled down in mountain tracts. The Rohela clan practised slave trade. A Rohel horse-man captures Guru Nanak and offers him for sale in the market. A Rohel Chief purchases Nanak in exchange for two Iraq horses. This Chief is called a Mir and is a Sufi. He easily finds that Nanak is a true *dervish*, a *fakir of* God. The Mir says to Nanak:—"Be merciful to me, O holy one!"

Nanak says to him:—"Thou hast captured so many and reduced them to slavery and tortured men and women. So hast thou forged chains for thee. Heavy is thy burden, O Mir!"

And the Mir says:—"Forgive me, O holy one! How may I be saved?"

Nanak says:—"O Mir! thou hast set the house on fire and art asleep in this house on fire! Release them all: spend all thou hast gained by evil means in the service of the poor, and abolish slavery."

And all the slaves are freed. And the Mir is a new man: he lives a simple life and invokes the Name of God.

*

It is a moon-lit night. And the Guru calls at the hut of a leper. The Guru says he would be the leper's guest for the night. The leper is wonder-struck. "Who are you?"—the leper asks. And the Guru sings a song and, as a bird that rests on a tree at night, but departs at dawn, so doth the Guru sing to the leper a song and, after singing it and blessing the leper, goes away. The song of Nanak lingers long in the heart of the leper. Nanak says:—

Sing the song of *Nama*!
And you will know that suffering comes
When we forget Him,—the Beloved!
Forgetfulness is the seed of suffering:
And suffering sets us on fire:

And we pass thro' a hundred fires,
Until we learn to sing the Name,
And fever dies down
And we are cool again!
So sing, brother leper, sing
The Song of the Name!

Pundits and priests meet him in Hardwar and say to him:—"What is your caste? And of what town are you?" And meekly answers the Guru:—"My caste is the caste of wood and fire, and I come from a town whence come both day and night!"

Kartarpur Community

Guru Nanak was a lover of the village-folk. He sang in the sweet vernacular of the villages,—the Punjabi. Guru Nanak's songs, in the Punjabi, were the beginning of a new renaissance in the Punjab: in these songs was the seed of Punjabi literature. The Guru's songs were taken up by wandering *fakirs*: they carried the sweet verses in the vernacular in their travels, from place to place. In Sikh temples, too, some opened village schools, where students learnt by heart the *Gur-bani*,—the songs of Guru Nanak in Punjabi.

Guru Nanak was a lover, too, of the soil. On his return from his far-off travels, he settled down at Kartarpur as a farmer: he was a lover of the peasant and the simple folk.

Nanak, the farmer-teacher, found the key to life in labour, poverty, silence, prayer and service of the people. Nanak started, at Kartarpur, the *langar* (the common kitchen) where bread was free to all. Bread is the Lord's and the bread which the Lord giveth is a *prasad* (God's grace). "Bread and water belong to the Guru," they said. And the Beloved, the Guru said, is in the People!

Crowds of his disciples came,—from Kabul and Central Asia, from Assam and Southern India. The Afghan and the Baloch, the

Turk and the Tartar, the Sufi and the Brahmin mingled, one with the other, to cultivate the wheat farms at Kartarpur: and he, their spiritual Father moved slowly on foot, labouring in the farm and singing Hymns of *Nama* and breathing out on all the benediction of Love!

Nanak's group worshipped God without pomp, without show, amid the silence of nature. And they,like their great leader, the Guru, served the poor. Kartarpur radiated selflessness. Guru Nanak was a picture of humility: and his comrades, in a spirit of true discipleship, worked as humble servants of the poor. From Kartarpur spread the fire of a new love of God and man all over the Punjab. Guru Nanak's face shone with the simplicity and peace of a saint who was, also, a labourer a toiler, a servant of the poor and lowly. Work and worship, love and labour, silence and song were blended together in the life at Kartarpur.

Guru Nanak, at Kartarpur, cultivated a triple silence. He merged himself in (1) the silence of God, the *Sat Nama*, the Eternal Word; (2) the silence of Nature, the silence that shines in the starry sky and dwells in the lonely hill and the flowing river; and (3) the fellowship of the *Sangat*, the Community of believers and *sewaks*, that stayed with the Guru and whom he called his "brother" (*bhais*).

The Community in Kartarpur, drinking in the inspiration of Guru Nanak's presence, learnt, more and more, to purify their hearts for worship of the One Infinite, and service of the poor. The life of blended prayer and service, to which the Kartarpur Community was called, underminded, in a natural way, egoism and self-idolatory. The Community shone with a radiance of the deifying light which God pours out upon His *bhaktas* and dedicated servants.

The influence and the example of Guru Nanak's life leavened the Punjab invaded, alas! by Moghul armies. The Kartarpur Community lived a simple life of prayer and service, a hidden life of labour and solitude. Guru Nanak's teaching of humility,—the fundamental note of his life,—was written out before the Community in the farm the Guru cultivated and the *langar* the Guru nourished with his love and devotion. At Kartarpur, the Guru and his Comrades lived united to God in love and united to man in the service of love.

"Let But The Flowers Remain Fresh!"

Bright was the day and beautiful the hour, when he, who was the brother of life and the brother of death, the brother of all humanity and the brother of all creation, passed away.

The smile, the light from within, that shone in his face, went not out in the hour of his departure.

It was the year of grace 1539, when, in the holy colony of Kartarpur, Guru Nanak prepared to depart.

By him is his beloved disciple, Lehna,—the son of a rich man who once dressed in the yellow silk of Bukhara but who now, as a disciple of the Guru, is become a picture of simplicity, and wears rough *khadi*, and works in the Guru's farm, and gladly lifts on his head heavy loads of wet grass, and serves the Guru, day and night, spending his money in the service of the poor and the *Sangat*. Lehna has been transformed into an image of his Guru. The word "lehna," in Punjabi, means "what is due to one from another." And the Guru had said to him:—"Thy *lehna* is from me: I have to pay thee: wander no more, O Lehna! I now call thee `Angad.' Thou art a limb of my body, a breath of my being,—one with me in the Spirit, blended with my soul," And now the day is come when Nanak is about to depart: in humility and love, Nanak bows to his disciple, Angad. What a moving sight!

Nanak came into the world singing, we are told, and Nanak departs singing. Nanak's life, on earth, was a Song of Heaven: and now Nanak leaves the earth with a song on his lips. St. Francis, on the day of his departure, said to Elias:—"Suffer me, Brother, to rejoice in my Lord: by the grace of His Spirit, I feel so united to Him that I needs must sing." And St. Francis sang the "Song of the Sun," the Canticle in "Praise of the Creatures,"—the Song filled, through and through, with the message of joy for all mankind. Guru

Nanak sings a song of joy in the hour of his departure. Guru Nanak sings "The Wedding Song":—

Sing ye, my comrades! sing!
Sing, now, my Wedding Song!
Sing ye the Song of His praise!
Sing the Song of Him, my Lord:
Let me be a sacrifice
To His Wedding Song.

The blessed day hath dawned:
The hour of wedding is come:
Come! comrades, come!
Await the bride!
And the oil of your blessings pour on her:
For she, the bride, doth meet her Lord!

Many of Nanak's disciples shed tears, and some ask him:— "Master! what rites shall we observe?" So had some asked him, years ago:—"Master! shall we light the lamp and offer *pinda* and *pattal* as cakes of oblation, when you have departed? And shall we throw your ashes and your bones into the waters of the Ganges?" The Guru, then, had answered thus:—

Yes! Light the Lamp! But let it be
The Lamp of the Name of God!
This Lamp giveth Light.
And my *pind* and *pattal* shall be God!
Let my funeral rites be,—*smaran*,
Remembrance of the Name of God!
For He, the Lord, alone
Is my support, here and in the hereafter.
Sing the Name of God!
That shall be my Ganges and my Kashi:
Let my soul bathe in the Ganges of His Name!
True bath is his who has in his heart
The Love of God, night and day!
And let my *pinda*-cakes to be grace of God!

So, when, in the hour of his departure, his Hindu disciples ask him:—"Shall we cremate your body?" and his Muslim disciples ask:—"Shall we bury the body?" he says—"Quarrel not! Let Hindus bring flowers and place them on one side of the body: let Muslims bring flowers and place them on the other side. Then let each group do what it likes, if but the flower remain fresh!"

Indifferent was the Guru of cremation or burial: he only asked that the flowers remained fresh,—the flowers of faith and love. Centuries have passed since the day Guru Nanak left his earth-body here and entered into the Abode of Light,—the *Satya-loka*: and we, alas! still quarrel over outer matters of rites and ceremonies, forgetting the teaching of the Guru:—"Let these be what you will, if but the flowers of faith and love remain fresh."

Alas! they looked for the Guru,—Some in grave, some on the cremation ground: they looked for the Living, the imperishable among the passing, the evanescent. The Living Guru is not in them who cling to this sect or that, this ceremony or that, this book or that, this temple or that creed. The Living Guru is in the hearts of those whose flowers of faith and love are fresh. For he came for all.

He founded no sect: he revered all religions. He taught no creed: he preached love and noble deed. He proclaimed that all the people were the people of God. In the Hindu, as in the Muslim, he saw the vision of Man. In all castes he saw the one sacred Brotherhood of Humanity. In all the nations he beheld the procession of the one Race of love,—the one Race of Humanity. To all countries and to all peoples he sang the "song of *Nama*." Therefore, as his disciple, Bhai Gurdas, sang:—"Humanity resounds with his hymns, and he makes our hearts gardens of love and peace: and rivers flow in us, singing his songs." Therefore, has Nanak a throne in the hearts of men. His Teaching is a Song of the immortals: and this Farmer has planted, in many aspiring hearts, the seed of a new faith, a new vision, a new life. As a disciple of the great Guru sings:—"The seed is of God and the seed is growing!"

Kabir: The Weaver-Singer

THE WORD "*kabir*" occurs in Hindi literature and means "great." A truly great one, indeed, was Kabir. The word "*kabir*," also, occurs in the poetry of the great Sindhi poet, Shah Latif.

Surdas, Tulsi and Kabir are among the greatest, names in Hindi literature. The supreme poet of Hindi literature is Tulsi,-almost a contemporary of Shakespeare. Tulsi was adopted by a *rishi*, a forest mystic. And Tulsi wrote the matchless story of Sri Rama in matchless Hindi. His book, the "Rama Charit Manas," reciting the deeds of Sri Rama, was regarded by Mahatma Gandhi as "the greatest book in all devotional literature."

surdas was, like Homer, blind. This blind poet of Agra wrote remarkable poems on the life and adventures of Krishna.In his poems is a deep spirit of *bhakti* or devotion. In one of them he sings of the soul's mystic separation from the Divine Spouse, -Krishna,- thus:-

> Mine eyes rain tears, night and day:
> For me 'tis the rainy season alway:
> For Shyam Sunder is away!

Surdas was born in 1483. Kabir was born in 1440. Tulsi came much later, being born in 1532. A careful student of the literatures of India, Sir George Grierson,ventures to regard Tulsi as "the most important figure in the whole of Indian literature."

It cannot be denied that these three poets,-Sur, kabir and Tulsi,- appeared in a trying period of India's history. *Satya yuga*, with its emphasis on the inner life, had long disappeared. *Kali yuga* had set in, as a part of the cycle of time. And *kali yuga*, with its emphasis on the outer world and outer life, had dragged the Indian people far away from the spiritual vision of India's *rishis*. These three great poets sang poems of the Inner Life and the Spiritual Vision of India: they sang from the very depths of the heart. Kabir's is a song of the heart. His religion is that of the heart. His message is, essentially, a message of the purified and emancipated heart.

Kabir, a simple weaver of Banaras, had place in his heart for both the Hindu and the Muslim. He was fascinated by the teaching of Ramananda. And though brought up in a Muslim home, he became a devotee of Rama and wrote poems of rare beauty to interpret his religion of the heart, which recognised no temples, no mosques, no idols, no castes, but only God.

When I think of Kabir, I love to think of him as a weaver with a delicate and smiling face, as a mystic with sparkling eyes. I never think of Kabir as an ascetic with a pale, emaciated face. I love to think of him as a singer of joy. kabir was a child of music.

In kabir I behold a free, radiant spirit, sending out the love of his heart to Hindus and Muslims alike, to all creatures. including birds and beasts. He has an emotion of tenderness for the entire creation. To kabir the universe is a swing in which the Lord of creation sits with His creatures to play with them the *leela* of joy. In one of his poems, Kabir sings thus;-

> God dances in rapture:
> And when His great joy
> Touches the body and the mind,
> They cannot contain themselves.
> He holds all that is
> Within His Eternal bliss!

Kabir surveyed the situation around him and he saw Hindus and Muslims quarrelling with one another in the name of religion. He realised that religions, which quarrelled with one another, were no better than creeds. Religions, he realised, to be a source of blessings, must reconcile, not fight,-must bring together, not antagonise. He saw the *pundit* and the *moulvi* daily fighting with one another. He realised that a new, renovated Indian society required a new religion,-one of brother hood and peace and love.

In song after song, Kabir sang of this religion of love. In song after song was an invocation of a new sermon on the mount, a new voice of compassion and brotherhood. In one of his songs are the following moving words:-

> I am a child of Ram and Allah:
> I accept all gurus and pirs

O God,-whether called Allah or Ram,-
I live by Thy holy Name!

*

What avails it
To wash your mouth,
To count your beads
To bathe in holy streams,
To bow in temples,
If, while you mutter your prayers,
Or go on pilgrimages,
Purity is not in your heart?

No wonder the *brahmins* were infuriated. Some of them sent a courtesan to tempt him. But he blessed her and she became his disciple. In Banaras, the number continued to increase of those who criticised Kabir and abused him. How patiently he bore it all! To be patient in the midst of persecution, to smile and be serene when others chastise you,- there is the secret of the true joy which sings in the poems of Kabir.

Picture after picture rises before my mind as I think of this simple weaver of Kashi. He weaves at his loom and earns his daily bread and, day after day, he serves the humble and the simple, offering food and cloth, offering bread and water to them,in such a simple, loving way that they cling to his lotus-feet. The proud of purse persecute him: but the poor ones bless him. He calls them "the poor of Rama." Kabir is devoted, with the beautiful love of his kingly heart, to the poor and simple ones. With what joy they meet him! With what joy the peasants and the poor ones come to him and receive the benediction of his blessed heart! Kabir is a lover of the poor; Kabir is a spiritual communist: Kabir is a worshipper of the God of the broken ones.

Kabir's ethic was simple. He taught:-

(1) Live justily. Be sincere. sincerity is the foundation of true religious life. Drive deceitfulness out of your hearts.

(2) Forget not that God, the Supreme, is a Being whom you cannot chain in words and creeds. "He is a Nameless Being," says Kabir, "of whom nought can be said." Who can describe Him by

the words of the mouth? Who can write Him on paper? Feel Him!Taste Him! And you may know how sweet He is. But you cannot explain Him. Can a dumb person, who tastes a sweet thing, explain how sweet it is? So avoid controversies in matters spiritual. Kabir warns against creeds and controversies. Drink thy Lord in silence! is the teaching emphasised by him, again and again.

This teaching of Kabir,-a re-wording of the teaching of the "Upanishads,"-influenced India's great king, one of the greatest kings of all centuries, Akbar when he said:-"Each person, according to his condition, gives the Supreme Being a Name, but in reality to name the supreme is vain." Yes,-for the Supreme is Nameless.

Kabir, like the great poet of South India, Vamana, spoke disapprovingly of castes and pilgrimages. That poet wrote:-"Why do you constantly revile the pariah? Are not his flesh and blood the same as our own? And does not He pervade the pariah? And of what caste is He?" So taught Kabir, also.

(3) Go within and meet thy God who greets thee in the heart! Listen to kabir's own ravishing words:-

I laugh when I hear
That the fish in the water is thirsty!
Why wander ye when the water of life
Is within you?

*

How sad to think that you go,
From forest to forest, in search
Of what is within you!

*

Go where you will,
To Kashi or to Mathura,
What do you gain if you do not see
The vision within you?

*

O my heart! to what shore would you cross?
The Shoreless Infinite

Is within you!

*

Go where you will:
Where will you find the place
That may quench the thirst of your souls?
The waters of life
Are within you!

*

Be strong! Be brave!
Be heroic!
Enter in silence
Within you!

*

And keep your foothold firm!
Ponder well on these words, O my heart!
And look within you!

*

Go not elsewhere!
Put all imaginations away!
Stand fast in what you really are!
And behold what you really are.
Within you!

*

No wonder such songs of bewitching beauty pased from mouth to mouth and ravished the hearts of Kabir's countrymen, Hindus and Muslims alike. No wonder, when this great singer and saint passed on, Hindus and Muslims contended for his body. the Hindus saying, "We shall burn it;" the Muslims saying, "We shall bury it!" And the dispute between them rose to a pitch of hot controversy, when some one, wiser perhaps than the rest, raised the cloth that covered the body. When, lo and behold! they saw but heaps of flowers! The body had vanished: only the flowers remained! And some flowers the Hindus took and burnt them in

Banaras: and some flowers the Muslims took and buried them in Maghar.

But the songs of this singr of the Secret shining in the heart within passed on from mouth to mouth among the people. And the songs of Kabir sang again in the heart of him, who came from Kabir's own country of the Soul: the songs re-sang in the heart of Guru Nanak. And Kabir and Nanak blended into one and in matchless melody made a music of the Holy Spirit that moveth in the heart within!

It is this Religion.- of the spirit,-which India needs today, this Religion of Love, not the materialistic communism of the West,- this Religion of the Heart, which India, in the coming days, will pass on to the Nations as a gift from Kabir and Nanak and the great galaxy of India's saints and *fakirs* and singers of love and compassion. It is the Religion of the Heart which includes and transcends the religion of works. This Religion of the Heart will blend action with silence and prayer. This religion of the Heart will teach that the chanting of words in temples or mosques is of little value compared to the true prayer of service and sacrifice. This Religion of the Heart, renouncing the externals of worship, will turn away from the temples and the mosques and the churches, which are untrue to the law of poverty and renunciation, when they amass wealth in the face of hunger and starvation around. and this Religion of the Heart, as Kabir taught again and again, will be the Religion of mercy to all creatures.

Implanted deep in the heart of Kabir was compassion for all creatures. And he made it a rule that abstinence from flesh diet was incumbent on everyone who would be a member of his *satsang* or community.

Kabir heard the voice of suffering. The vibrations of an invisible lyre seemed to descend on his soul from the very stars. "Kill not creatures," he said; "and do not make the flesh an article of your food!" Kabir felt that in touching the creature, he was touching God. To kabir, as to St. Francis, birds and beasts were brothers and sisters. He greeted them and poured upon them the love of his heart. Kabir was bred in a Muslim family: yet to him the cow was sacred and every creature was sacred.

To three things, primarily, was Kabir's life dedicated:-(1) service of the poor; (2) manual labour, work by the hand; and (3) singing "*Ram-Nam*" from the depths of the heart to the Beloved who shineth in the heart within.

The greatest of Kabir's disciples was Dhani Dharamdas. He was a rich merchant and he spent his wealth(i) in spreading the faith of his Master; (ii) in the service of widows and orphans, of prisoners and pilgrims,- and he did it all in a spirit of joy; (iii) and out of the depths of joy in his heart he, too, sang songs of wondrous beauty,-songs to the Beloved.

Orthodox priests and orthodox *mullahs*, alas! opposed Kabir. Kabir, who was a preacher of peace, not hatred, who endeavoured to unite classes and communities, Hindus and Muslims, in the one service of God and the people, felt that his presence in Kashi was an eye-sore to many influential people. Kabir felt he should peacefully leave kashi. When he actually was leaving Kashi for Maghar, to spend there the last days of his life, how the people,- the poor and afflicted ones,-crowded together to touch his blessed feet! Some tried to induce him to stay in kashi. He opened his arms to embrace them, then went on his way of silent service and healing, saying:-"Sri Rama calleth me to Maghar. May you all live in the Light of Rama! To Him I go. Forget not that in Maghar is He and He is in Kashi, too! And may He bless you all!"

Is not Kabir a Voice of the Ancient Wisdom? I know not what would have become of the religion of the *rishis* if Kabir and Nanak and Dadu Dayal and Rajab and the Sikh Gurus and a few others, who appeared in the Dispensation of saints and *bhaktas* had not renewed it and restored it to its place in the heart of Hindusthan? Through their lives and teachings they renewed the inner life of India and, inspired by the truth of reconciliation, brotherhood and love, they transformed the social life of countless men and women. Kabir and nanak became prophets of a new Religious Renaissance. And Nanak's followers passed on the torch of this New Renaissance to many countries. The torch was aflame for more than three centuries and still flickers in the hearts of many *bhaktas* and seekers of God. And I can but trust that this New Renaissance will not be lost in the secular movements of today, but will continue ever more and more to grow in the New Epoch that awaits us.

"Who Is My Father?"

Kabir I regard as one of the world's great prophets of pure spiritual life. And spiritual life asks for purification from extraneous elements, from all forms of compromise with the mass-man, from creeds and conventions. Pure spirituality is liberated spirituality. So we may understand why Kabir taught "*Rama-Nama*" and bhakti or love in the heart. Kabir sttached little value to asceticism of the body, to pilgrimages and other practices of "popular" religion.

Kabir speaks of a five-old renunciation:-

(1) Renounce comfort! Live the simple life!

(2) Renounce scriptures! "They do not take you far," says Kabir. "Scholars," he says, "have gone astray, though they have read the Vedas. They know not the secret of the Self."

(3) Renounce pride! *Sat-Karma* (good deeds), indeed, helps the aspirant to spiritual life. Good deeds are reallly meant to wear off the *rajas* in us. The *rajasic* quality must be exhumed. Hence the need of *sat-Karma*. But often *sat-karma* only develops pride (*ahankara*) in us. and pride must go, if you will grwo in the life of the Spirit. Pride is destroyed through the Name of the Lord. "God's Name," says Kabir, "is the breaker of pride! Listen to what he says!

> Your good deeds may be many:
> But, alas! you are consumed with pride.
> He, whose Name is the breaker of pride,
> How can he congratulate you on your good deeds.
> Which only feed your pride?
> They who give up all pride.-
> Pride of caste and. birth and race,-
> And they who renounce attachment
> And seek alone the Word Divine within,-
> They move onward to the goal!

(4) Renounce desire! It is the seed of sin. Kabir says:-

They who renounce the seed
Of all desire. all hot willing,-
They are freed form body and space,
And they pass into the freedom of timelessness!

(5) Renounce *moha* (attachment)! All *moha* is rooted in desire. kabir says:-

They who renounce attachment
And seek alone the Word Divine within,-
They attain to the Supreme!

Kabir's mother, Nima, reproaches him, one day. His father, Nur Ali or Niroo, is dead. The family must be looked after. Kabir has spent his time in singing the Name of Rama. The mother, Nima. cannot bear to see her children starve. She reproaches Kabir on his neglect.

"What are you doing, my son?" she says. "Your father has gone. There is none else to look after the family, if you will not wake up. Open your eyes and do your weaving."

Then says Kabir to her, in a beautiful poem enshrined in the "Guru Granth Saheb":-

say, who is son?
Who is father.
And uncle who?
In separation from Hari,
How shall I live, O mother?
No longer can the world deceive me;
For I have known the deceiver (maya)!

And Kabir continues:—

My God! Compassionate art Thou to the poor!
I trust in Thee!
And all my family have I put in the boat:
Let it float on!

Kabir's mother sobs and weeps. She says:-"O Allah! how shall my children live? Kabir hath given up his weaving. Kabir inscribes Rama's Name on his body!"

Yes,-Kabir has no *moha* "Who is my father? Who is my mother?" asked Jesus. "Who is my mother?"is also the cry of Kabir's emancipated heart. "Who is son, and who is father, and uncle who?"In answer to Nima's loud lament, kabir answers thus, in a beautiful song which, also, you may find in the "Guru Granth Saheb":-

Yes, mother! while the thread
Was passing through the bobbin,
I forgot my Beloved God.
Yes, mother! my understanding is poor
And my caste is that of weaver.
But this I know, mother!
Losing in money,
I have gained the Name of God!
Hear, O mother! hear!
The One God will provide for us all!

The Triple Secret

Kabir was illiterate but illuminated. In this regard, he reminds us of the great western mystic, Boehme. Kabir was, essentially, a man of interior illumination But he was, as Boehme was not, a great musician and a great poet. Kabir was, also , an expert craftsman. He made his living at the loom. In this regard, he reminds us of Raidas. Kabir was a simple weaver as Raidas was a simple cobbler.

Kabir was not an ascetic. He did not leave the world. His renunciation was inner, not outer. He mingled as a man with men: he toiled, he recognized the sanctity of labour and he rejoiced in the interior life of communion with the Supreme.

Kabir blended nystical vision with industry. He believed in the harmony of hands and heart. And the more I think of him, the more I feel that Kabir had a natural dislike for institutional religion, for all externalism. In this regard, he reminds me of the Quakers of England, who believe in the "Inner Light." Kabir spoke, again and again, of "simple union with God." He sang of "*sahaj samadh*," simple union, the "*samadh*" of the simple heart. Kabir did not attach value to pilgrimages. "Not in Ka'aba nor in Kailash, but in thy heart within mayst thou meet thy Lord," he says. One of his songs has the significant words:-

> Where dost thou seek me?
> Lo! I am beside thee!
> Neither in temple nor in mosque am I:
> Neither in Ka'aba nor in Kailash!
> I am not in outer rites and ceremonies.
> I am by thee, with thee, within thee!

"Do not tell me," says kabir, "that the saints of God belong to this caste or that." The saints transcend all castes, all countries, all creeds. Hath not God revealed Himself in different castes and different faiths? Barbers and washermen, carpenters and masons, sweepers and cobblers have communed with God, face to face! So Kabir asks us to recognise the value of home-life for spiritual advance.

He sings:-

> Lamps burn in every home.
> Thy Lord is within thee:
> Why climb the palm tree to seek Him?
> The telling of beads is nought to him!

Kabir raised his voice against those who identified religion with externalism. Of the interior life, he spoke in rapturous strains, again and again. Misled, he says, is the man who, leaving home, wanders afar.?Call back, says Kabir, call back the wanderer home. And Kabir urges, again and again, that the Home of homes "is in the heart within."

Kabir did not stand aloof from life and its obligations. To him life itself was a revelation of the Real. Kabir was a singer of life."In life," he says, "deliverance abides." Here and now mayst thou find thy God! Not in a far-off forest, but here, in thy daily life, mayst thou greet thy God, if thou wilt but awake.

In one of his poems, he says:-

> If your bonds be not broken
> Now and here, in this earthly life,
> What hope is there for deliverance for you in death?

And again:-

> If God is found now, He is found in death and beyond.
> If you find Him not now, you but go to dwell
> In the City of Death.

Kabir emphasises the value of the immediate. Precious is your life. Do not waste it in distraction, but so live that you may find Him before death overcomes you. God is now, here, or He is nowhere! Do not, therefore, miss the golden chance this life gives you for self-realisation. Here is pure water before you. Drink it in. Be filled: Why do you pursue the shadowshapes which come and go? Why do you wander after the mirage? The "water of life" is before you. Listen to the words of Kabir:-

> Dhruva, prahlada and Sukdeva
> Have drunk of the nectar:
> And Raidas, the cobbler, too.
> Listen to me, brother!
> Weave no longer your chains of falsehood!
> Hold no longer the load of desire on your head!
> Be light, if thou wouldst, indeed, be liberated!

How may I be light? Kabir's answer is significant. (1) Be detached. And (2) be true,-no matter what suffering you may have to pass through. Be true, though persecuted by men, though assailed by suffering and pain. Bear witness to the truth. And (3)be thirsty for love. This triple secret,-detachment, worship or truth and thirst of love,-is the key to that higher life to which all awakening must aspire as its crown. "The saints." says Kabir, "are drunk with love."

The secret of the *Prem Nagar*, the City of Love, was seen by Kabir. He lived a life of detachment; he adored truth, day by day, and his heart was filled with love. Thinking of him, I say to myself, what a joy in the thought that in this world of strife and pain, this world of conflict and contradiction, this broken world of tragedy and tears, have appeared, again and again, singers and seers like Kabir who saw the Secret of the Beauteous Face of the Beloved.

The Little Way

Bayazid was a *sufi*, a *fakir*, a *dervish* of God. and of him, one day, they ask:- "master! how old are you?

And the *sufi* saint answers:-"Four years am I."

"How can that be?" they ask.

And he answers:-"My God was concealed from my soul by the conspiracy of the world for seventy years: but I have glimpsed a little of the beauty of God during the last four years, and they are the years which count as the period of my life."

The conspiracy of the world is the action of *maya*. It throws a veil upon us: and God, the great Reality, the only Reality of life, is concealed from our souls. The *guru* removes the veil. The guru is the veil-withdrawer. The *guru* is he who lifts the curtain. Hence the very first step to be taken by a sincere seeker is, as I have urged again and again, search for the *guru*. The *guru* is the lift to raise us to the heights, —the lift which may take us, little ones to the *Satya-loka* (the Realm of the Supreme). And os the Disciple's Way must needs be understood by every seeker after the Life Divine. In the teaching of Kabir, the Disciple's Way is indicated thus:-

(1) One thing emphasised by Kabir, over and over again, is longing (*pyas*). The disciple should become a *pyasi*, should grow in longing, before he can truly profit by the teaching of the *guru*.

(2) Again, he who would be a disciple must learn "renunciation." Dharamdas, the greatest disciple of Kabir, was a very rich man. He "renounced" his wealth, spent it in spreading the message of his

guru. Tyaga (giving up) is essential to the life of him who takes *saranam* (refuge) at his guru's feet.

(3) Thirdly, there is, in Kabir's *bani*, emphasis on *seva* (service). By *seva* is meant service of the *guru* and of the *sadhus* (pure ones) and of the Community (*satsang*), in whom the disciple sees his *Guru* reflected. *Seva* reflects itself naturally in objective acts. But the interior spirit of *seva* is humility. It is the secret of true holiness to which the true seeker aspires.

And what is humility? In its perfect flowering, humility is self-abnegation emptying out of all "self," all ego. The true disciple serves his master, day and night, and yet never feels that he has served. He says to himself:- "I have done nothing, for I am nothing."

(4) Then there comes into the life of the disciple a strange, joy-filling experience. The disciple feels the grace of God moving upon him. The grace of the *guru* to him is the grace of God Himself. The disciple, in this strange experience, feels the thrill of what true love is,-the love of the *guru* and the love of God. The disciple, at this stage, realises that the true vocation of life is love. "I shall be love," he says to himself. And the way of love is not to scramble for "great" things. The way of love is the little way. In ittle things, in simple things, in lowly things of life, the disciple knows, is his destiny fulfilled. And the aspiration within him grows from more to more:-"May I be little!May I grow, more and more, a little one!"

The joy which comes to the true disciple, to him who has learnt to walk the little way, the way of love, the way of *guru-bhakti* and *guru-seva*, is indescribable. Kabir's greatest disciple, Dharamdas, in his *bani* (Poems), has a beautiful little *sloka* in which he gives us an inkling of what this joy is:-

> The guru hath filled me with joy:
> I was sinking in the sea of worldliness:
> The guru held me by the arm and saved me!
> The guru blessed me and I was released
> From bondage to the Wheel of Birth and Death!

Mira: The Divine Singer

Of The Race Of Heroes

HOW RICH IS India's heritage! From the civilisation of the Sindhu,-the Indus Valley,-to the India of the twentieth century is a period which covers about six thousand years. During these centuries, India has thrown up men and women who have lived consecrated lives as servants of God and Man. Prophets and saints have, century after century, appeared in this Ancient Land. One of them was Mira.

Gujerat, Rajasthan and Hindusthan alike claim her as their poet and saint. They salute her as a singer of Sri Krishna. Her life was one white flame of *bhakti,* devotion to the Lord. The deepest cry of her heart,-was it not the very cry of him who said:- "As the hart panteth after the water-brooks, so panteth my soul after Thee, O Lord"?

Nabhaji, the great chronicler and interpreter of the devotees of Sri Rama and Sri Krishna, has some beautiful lines which indicate the very secret of the hold of Mira on the hearts of the Indian people. Nabhaji writes:-

> The trumpet of *bhakti* (love) she did blow,
> And of none was she afraid!
> The thought:-"What will they say?"
> She flung aside;
> She lost herself in devotion to the Lord!

The dates of her birth, marriage and death continue to be subjects of controversy among scholars.

Among the well-known poets and singers of God in India are (1) Namdev, in the tenth century, in the Maharashtra; (2) Chandidas, in the fourteenth century, in Bengal; (3) Lala, in the fourteenth century, in kashmir; (4) Vidyapati, in the fifteenth century, in

Mithila; (5) Kabir, in the fifteenth century, in the U.P.; (6) Narsing Mehta, in the fifteenth century, in Gujerat; (7) Mira, in the sixteenth century, in Rajasthan;(8) Sur Das, in the sixteenth century, in the U.P. and (9) Tukaram, in the seventeenth century, in the Maharashtra.

The "Guru Granth Saheb," the "Sikh Bible," belongs to the sixteenth-seventeenth century, and the "Ramayana" of Tulsi Das, described as the "Bible of Modern India," belongs, too, to the sixteenth-seventeenth century.

To the eighteenth century belongs Ramprasad Sen, the great Bengali singer of Kali, whom he invokes, as did Sri Ramakrishana Paramahansa in the twentieth century, as the "Mother." Ramprasad Sen is a *bhakti*-poet like Mira. There is not a village in Bengal where his songs are not sung. In the following little song, Ramprasad Sen sings with deep *bhakti* and spiritual insight:-

Mother!
This day, too, will pass,
And only rumour remain!
I came to the market of the world,
I sat by its bathing-ghat,
I sat down to sell my wares.

Mother!
The sun is seated on high,
And the Ferryman has come:
The load of many doth fill the Boat:
Alas! none thinketh of this unhappay one:
I am left behind,
For they ask for a coin from this poor man;
Where shall I get it?

Mother!
O Mother!
Give me, too, a place in the Boat!
Thy glory shall I sing!
And with Thy Name

And Thy Song on my lips
I shall plunge into the sea of life!

In the sixteenth century, India listened to the songs of a number of Hindi poets, who all worshipped at the one shrine of the love of God and man. One of these was this great woman-singer, Mira. Yet another great poet associated with the same century was Tulsi.

Sur Das and Mira Bai are the greatest Krishna-poets in Hindi, Namdev and Tukaram are the greatest in Marathi, and Narsing Mehta is a master-singer of Krishna in Gujerati.

Sur Das if often referred to as "the blind bard of Agra." Was he born blind? Or did he become blind at a later period? Or does he call himself "blind" figuratively? I do not know. He himself said that Krishna's vision came to him and. thereafter, all was "darkness" to him. Yes.-the vision of the Lord so filled him, that *samsara* (the world) lost all attraction for him. The world became to him a vale of "darkness."

Tulsi is, indeed, a very great, name in Hindi literature: he sang of Rama, as Mira sang of Krishna. There are some who regard Tulsi as the prince of Hindi poets. Sir George Grierson, a great student of Indian languages, says that "Tulsi Das is the brightest star in the firmament of Hindi literature."

One thing Tulsi and Mira had in common. They both put emphasis on the value of *Nama*, the Name Divine. The Name to Tulsi, was Rama. The Name, to Mira, was shyama. yet Mira, too, refers, in some of her lyrics,to Rama as the Name Divine.

"Remember His Name," says Tulsi. "This," he adds "is the royal road to salvation." As Mira is never tired of singing the Name of Krishna or Shyama, so is Tulsi tireless in singing of *Rama-Nama*. "*Rama-Nama*." he says, "is to my heart as water is to the fish." And both Tulsi and Mira use in their Hindi many words which are taken from Brija-bhasha,-the language which Sri Krishna used in the long ago.

All the three,-Sur, Tulsi and Mira,-are *bhakti*-poets of a very high order. The holy man, according to Tulsi, is he who sings *Nama*, the Name Divine. "He ever sings," Tulsi says, "the Holy

Name." And

From place to place
He wandereth still,
To give to men the knowledge
That illumines and purifies!
Blessed, indeed, is the land
Where dwell such holy ones.
Love is the law of their life:
Helpers are they,-and healers.
Their senses are subdued,
Their thoughts do dwell
On none but the Lord.
To the One are they devoted, ever true!
And in their hearts they know
The world is but a dream.
And as the cuckoo
Doth in rainy season long
For a drop of rain,
So long they for the Lord!

In these words of Tulsi is enshrined the very soul of *bhakti* which Mira sings in words no less enchanting. Mira places the flute on her lips and wears the *pitambar* (yellow cloth), which Krishna wore in Brindaban. And with a smile on her lips, Mira places her heart at the Lotus-feet of shyama. Then, with the little silver-bells on her feet and cymbals in her hands, she stands up in the presence of Shyama to sing:-

I have heard the Voice:
It saith:-"I come!"
I move from house to house
In quest, ye pilgrims on the Path!
When will He come,-
The King of my Heart?
When? O when?

Centuries have passed since these words were sung by Mira. Yet, even today, as we listen to them, they find an echo in our hearts.

Mira was famous for her beauty and her *bhakti* (devotion to Sri Krishna). "Her history," writes the English historian of Rajasthan, "is a romance." As brave as she was beautiful she wandered far and wide, from the Ganga to Dwarka, visiting shrines of Sri Krishna and singing her songs filled with intense longing.

Mira is not merely a singer: she is one of the great heroines of Rajasthan. Persecuted by her brother-in-law, after the departure of her husband' Bhoj Raj, who loved her intensely, Mira flinches not an inch in her devotion to Sri krishna. She is full of the Rajput spirit of heroic resistance to injustice and opression.

Count Keyserling was a world-traveller and a great thinker. And this is what he wrote about Chitor:- "No place on earth has been the scene of equal heroism or knightliness or an equally noble readiness to die."

To a race of heroes and heroines belongs Mira. She renounces her all and leaves her palace in quest of her Beloved,-Sri Krishna. The words of Will Durant, the great interpreter of the history of civilisation, are so significant that I am tempted to quote them. The milltary spirit of the Rajputs enabled them, says Durant, "to defend themselves against the Moslems with historic valour." The story of the fall of Chitor, one of the Rajput, capitals, Durant says, "is as romantic as any legend of Arthur or Charlemagne. The Mohammedan invader, Alau-d-din, Durant points out, "wanted not Chitor but the princess Pudmini,- 'a title bestowed only on the superlatively fair.' The Moslem chieftain proposed to raise the siege if the regent of Chitor would surrender the princess Being refused, Alau-d-din agreed to withdraw if he were allowed to *see* pudmini. Finally he consented to depart if he might see Pudmini.in a mirror; but this too was denied him. Instead, the women of Chitor joined in defending their city; and when the Rajputs saw their wives and daughters dying beside them they fought until every man of them were dead. When Alau-d-din entered the capital he found no sign of human life within its gates; all the males had died in battle and their wives had burned themselves to death."

In a later period, when Akbar was the emperor of India, many a Rajput state surrendered to him, but the Rajput kingdom of Mewar remained independent. Mewar never compromised her honour, her independence or her religion. Mewar stood erect in the face of Islamic invasion. And Mewar remained as Col. Tod admits, "the sacred bulwark of religion."

"Where Is My Bridegroom?"

Mira comes to Sri Krishna through her mother. Standing on the roof of her house, one day, Mira sees a marriage procession and the bridegroom in the procession. The bridegroom is called "*dulaha*." Deeply impressed with the sight. Mira runs to her mother and asks:- "Mother! where is my *dulaha*"

And Mira's mother says offhand:-"Gridhara Gopal."

The word "*dulaha*" means not only "bridegroom" but, also, the "beloved."

From this day onward, Mira never forgets that her *dulaha* ,the "Beloved," is Girdhara Gopla, Krishna! From this day onward, Mira regards herself as the bride of Sri Krishna! And, every day, she thinks of Him: she builds an:Image of Shyama from the dust of the earth and, sitting in silence, looks at the Image, again and again. Absorbed in the one thought, the one vision of Shyama, is Mira every day.

Some days after this arrives in Mira's village a *sadhu.* He has with him a small Image of Gridhara Goplal. Mira sees that the *sadhu* worships this Image. And she runs to her mother, saying;- "Mother! get me that Image of Shyama."

The mother requests the *sadhu* if he would give the Image to Mira.

The *sadhu* saya: "Mother! Shyama is my *Ishta*, my Lord, to whom I offer daily worship. And wherever I go, I take this Image with me. Not for a single moment am I away from the Image. How can I give It to Mira?"

And Mira's mother reports to Mira what the *sadhu* has told her. At night, the sadhu has a vision of Sri Krishna in his sleep. Sri Krishana says to him:- "My devotee art thou: wilt thou not pass on

My Image to Mira?"

And early in the morning, the sadhu comes to Mira's house and gives the Image to Mira's mother, saying:- "To Mira I give this Image,-my richest treasure,-for the Lord hath so ordered me."

Krishna now is to Mira a living Holy Presence. Krishna is not to her a far-off God sitting somewhere in the clouds or a star. Krishna is become to Mira her Spouse, *dulaha*, her Beloved. The longing in her heart becomes deeper every day for union with Krishna. And she takes joy in renouncing her earthly things for the sake of her "Beloved."

At a very early age, Sri krishna puts His song in her mouth. She becomes a flute of the Lord. The orientation of her soul is every day towards Sri krishna. So is her life gradually transformed into an Image of the "Beloved." She is persecuted for her devotion to Shyama: but she remains calm. Persecuted by members of her own house, Mira becomes, more and more, a reflection of the beauty and love of Sri Krishna. Is not this a mark of the true *bhakta* of the Lord? The Gita calls it "*sthitapragna*. The wise man, though persecuted, remains calm: he is in communion with God.

A deep longing for the Lord inspires many of her lyrics. Some of them I have listened to, again and again, with tear-touched eyes. What a cry pierces the heart as you listen to the following song of Mira!

Beloved!
I wander still
In quest of Thee!
I am athirst
For Thy Eternal Love!
I long to make
My body a lamp,-
The wick where of will be
My tender heart.
And I would fill the lamp
With the scented oil
Of my love for Thee!
Then let it burn,
Day and night,

At thy shrine,
Beloved!

I can no longer bear
To be away from Thee.
Make me Thine own!
Make me like Thee!
And make me pure
As Thou art pure,
Beloved!

Through Darkness To Light

Mira was the only daughter of Ratan Singh, a brave Rajput prince, who fought the Moghul invader and , at last died on the battle-field. After Ratan Singh's death, Mira lived, in Merta, with her grandfather, Dudaji.

The dominant faith of Rajputana was devotion to Shiva: but Rana Dudaji was a devout Vaishnava. So was Mira brought up in the Vaishnava atmosphere.

The ruler of Mewar was Rana Sanga. His eldest son was Prince (Kanwar) Bhoj Raj. To him was Mira married. So great was Mira's *bhakti* for Krishna, that she took with her the Image of Sri Kfishna, which the *sadhu* had given her. Before this Image Mira would often sit and sing songs of thanks giving to Sri Krishna. She did not neglect her household duties. Her devotion to her husband was as keen as her *bhakti* for Krishna.

Soon after her marriage, Prince Bhoj Raj died. And Mira was filled with the spirit of *vairagya* (detachment,renunciation). Day and night, she would sit at Krishna's Feet and sing songs dedicated to the Lord. The one word on her lips was "Gopala." This word means "Guardian" of the Earth as, also, "Protector" of the Cow. Gradually, Mira grew, also, in the love of *sadhus* (servants of God). She served them with singular devotion.

The ruler of Mewar,-Mira's father-in-law, Rana Sanga,-died. He was succeeded by Rana Ratan singh, who was succeeded by Rana Vikramajit: it was he who sujbected Mira to many hardships. He had a bad temper, and he was not well-disposed to Mira. Day after day, was Mira persecuted. She bore it all in patience: she was dauntless in her devotion to Sri Krishna; in every difficult situation she found consolation in remembering the Lord.

The Rana asks her to give up *bhakti* for the Lord. Gentle yet firm, Mira continues to sing her songs of devotion. The Rana tells her to think of what the people will say. Mira's answer is:-"Let them say!" The Rana asks her to keep away from the company of the *Sadhus*. She tells the Rana to sit at their feet and purify himself.

Mira spends much of her time now in the Temple, specially built for her by her husband, Prince Bhoj Raj. Mira sings in the Temple: Mira dances before the Image of Sri Krishna. The Rana gets more and more annoyed; he sends to Mira her two lady-friends who ask her to give up singing and dancing and be obedient to the Rana. Mira's answer is:-

O friends!
Dyed deep am I
In the colour of Him
To whom I am consecrated,-
The colour of Krishna.

The two ladies are so deeply impressed with what Mira says that they themselves begin to sing and dance in Mira's company. They came to convert Mira: they stayed to sing and dance!

The Rana sends his sister, Uda Bai, to bring her round. Uda Bai, too, is converted and joins in the worship of Krishna, singing with Mira the Name of the Lord.

This irritates the Rana. He sends a cup of poison to Mira through a messenger who says to her:- "Mira! this is *amrita* (nectar):drink it!" The story has it, that she accepts the cup.

Uda Bai tells her:-"This is a cup of poison, Mira! Don't drink it!"

Mira says:- "I accept it as a cup of *amrita*."

She places the cup at the Feet of krishna, then drinks it. Mira remains unaffected!

The Rana is surprised, but does not yet understand. He declares:- "Mira shall not live! Mira shall not live!"

He sends her a basket, placing in it a serpent. "Mira!" says the Rana's messenger to her, "this basket is sent you by the Rana as a gift."

Once again Mira accepts it. She opens the basket Where is the serpent? She sees in the basket a picture of Sri Krishna! Not yet does the Rana understand. He continues to persecute Mira!

She now feels she whould not stay in the palace. She should be in a place where she may worship her Lord, unobstructed. She sends a letter to the great Saint, Tulsi Das. She asks him, if, indeed, she would not be justified in leaving the palace for some place where her mind may be at peace and where she may worship her Lord, undisturbed. Mira, in her letter to the Saint, writes:-

"They, of my own household, have combined against me and my difficulties are multiplied.

'Great is the trouble they give me in my endeavour to serve the *sadhus*,-the pure ones,-and to do *Kirtan*, singing Krishna's Name.

"O Saint of God! Thou art like my mother, my father: and thou art the giver of joy to *Hari-bhaktas*, devotees of Krishna.

"O tell me, what is right for me to do. Write to me that I may understand."

In answer to this, Saint Tulsi Das writes thus to Mira:-

"This be my conviction that He, Rama , is the dearest of all, worthy of all worship, the Breath of all breath, the one Beloved. To His Lotus-feet let me be devoted for ever!

On reading this letter, Mira rejoices and is now prepared to start for Brindaban. Her *sakhis* (sister-friends) feel very sorry. Uda Bai tries her best to persuade her not to go. To her and others Mira answers in a few words, filled with tenderness towards all and with longing for her Lord . The central note of her answer is:-"I shall be now a *vairagini* (homeless wanderer), singing the Name of Him who is the one Beloved,- who is my All."

Mira listens not to Uda Bai nor to any of her other friends. She quickly leaves the palace, singing the Name of the Beloved. The true *bhakta* never turns back. The true *bhakta's* watchword is, "onward!" Mira, devoted to her one Lord runs fast, leaving her palace and all worldly comforts behind. The midnight stars shine on her as she descends, step by step, and then wanders along the bank of the Ganges, crying,-"Shyama! Shyama!" The beauty of murmuring waters passes into her face, making it all the more beautiful.

Mira leaves Chitor, in the darkness of the night. Alone, she moves out. such, indeed, is ever the fate of those who would meet the Lord. They must tread the path alone!

This period is a difficult one in Mira's life. A difficult period, yes- and a blessed one. In this period it is that she passes through her destined "darkness of the soul."

Mira is a Rajput girl. Heroically, she moves out with love and longing in her heart. Heroically, she travels on the road alone. She passes through village after village. She blesses all who meet her. Boys and girls of cowherds come from many places to greet her, to serve her and be blessed by her. She moves on! In her heart is the Image of her Beloved alone.

A little prince said to some friends:- "Men cultivate thousands of roses in one garden. Yet they do not find what they seek, though they can find all they seek in a single rose or a single drop of water. They seek, but they find not, Their eyes are blind! The truly seek who seek with the *heart*."

Mira moves out alone on the path of quest, seeking with the *heart*, crying again and again:- "Where art Thou, Beloved?"

To understand the true import of Mira's songs, to enter into the depths of their meaning, is "to" note five stages in the path of Mira's quest:-

1. The awakening of the Self marked definitely by her question as a little girl:- "where is my dulaha (Beloved)?"

2. Realisation of the transitory nature of the world.

Mira says:- "The world is passing; my Beloved is All."

3. In the next stage, Mira passed through a period of "purification." It is, also. a period of intense mortification,- a period when sometimes she thinks the very heavens are falling. But she stands

firm. "Nothing short," she says, "nothing short of Thee, Beloved! I want not the world. Thou art my All!" This *mantra* she repeats, again and again:-"Thou, Beloved! art my All!"

4. Then comes tc Mira illumination, vision of the Lord,- the vision of Shyama in His beauty and His glory.

5. All these stages lead on to the final one,- the goal of the true *bhakta*'s life,- the stage of union. Her *trisna* (desire) vanishes. She no longer has a desire for any eathly thing. The "pilgrim" is spiritually blended with the "Beloved."

Is there not another stage, too, which comes after that of union? Is there not, in the case of some at any rate, the stage which we call the stage of "return to life"? In this stage, the self-realised person, the *bhakta* rejoices in the service of the Lord on this earth-plane of suffering and pain. The *bhakta* says:- "His grace has lifted me unto Him. Now must I return to them who are His, my Beloved's : they are in suffering and pain: I must serve them, and take up the cross that they may be sanctified."

After her rich "realisation" in her heart, Mira moves out among men to work for the Lord and be outpoured as an offering in the Flame of Sacrifice. And the highest work, the noblest se rvice, Mira realises, is *kirtan, Nam- kirtan*. Mira graduallly builds up groups of kindred spirits,- to sing the Name of the Lord.Mira's work is wonderful. It is not what is ordinarily understood by "work" Our "work,"- is it better than "utility" required by a community, a muscular and wage-earning society or state? Mira's "work" is "pure" work, pure act,-an offering to the Eternal. In this, the purest act, in *kirtan*, adoration of the Name, the cry of the soul is:- "No more worldliness! Thou, O Lord! Thou art my All!"

Krishna, Krishna, All Around !

Shrine after shrine does Mira visit as a wanderer and a pilgrim. To places of the holy ones Mira goes as a pilgrim to find escape, in the words of a great mystic, "from the flame of separation." "O

Krishna! Thou art my All!" is the deepest yearning of her heart. She wants not the world's wealth, neither palace nor paradise. She has longing for Krishna alone.

The one teaching of the great seers of humanity hath always been;- "Break all bondage of *moha* (attachment)!" This teaching Mira sings in number of her lyrics, as she wanders from place to place. In her heart burns a longing which is even as a fire consuming every thing worldly, every thing earthly, every thought even of "paradise,' The flame in her heart consumes every thing save the Beloved.

On her pilgrimage to shrine after shrine, she mees a number of men and women, and every word she speaks is an offering to Sri Krishna. Does she serve the needy as she moves on? Every act of her "service" is an offering to Sri krishna. Her offering is charged, through and through, with deep *shraddha* (faith or self-dedication to the Lord). Her pilgrimage is one rapturous procession, one wondrous song of adoration to the Lord.

In a significant *sutra* in Patanjali, we read the following pregnant words:- "He who sacrifices all to *Ishwara* (the Lord),-he enters into samadhi (the super-conscious state)" Mira has renounced her all to Him whom she loveth, so that nothing remains to her of her own. To Mira earthly things, all wealth, all worldly honours, all the joys of life in the palace are transient. Her only wealth and only joy is her Lord. And to Him she cries, again and again. Listen to some of Mira's deepest cries of the heart:-

Come, O Compassionate One!
Come and meet me, Master!
Mira is Thy maid-servant:
Through the ages
Hath Mira been Thine, Thine own!
Mira falls at Thy feet:
O bless me, Beloved!

Mira hath Thou accepted
As more than Thy maid.
Mira is Thy bride, Beloved!
Protect me then,

Guard Thou Mira's honour, Lord!
At Thy Lotus-feet
Do I shelter seek!
My refuge art Thou, Beloved!

And in this broad, boundless sea
Of life art Thou my Boat.
How can I cross
Without Thee, Beloved?

Many years have passed since I journeyed to see Mira's Temple at Chitor. Step by step, I ascended the height, until I reached Mira's shrine on that sacred evening which I may not easily forget. The sun had set. I entered the Temple. I bowed at the shrine with teartouched eyes.

Some one asked me:-"What is Mira?"

And I said:- "Sing on the Song of the Lord.-this is Mira!"

On her way onward, by day and by night, Mira sings on the Song of the Lord. And, as she sings, her eyes are touched with tears. Mira sings: Mira weeps: Mira cries:-"Where art Thou, Beloved?"

The pebbles of the road are pure after the rains. And the heart is purified after the rain of tears. Mira, with a strong, unearthly longing in her heart, cries out, again and sgain:-"Where art Thou. Beloved?"

Seeing a shrine at some distance Mira hails Krishna, agian and again:-"Beloved!" "Beloved!"

And moving on, she finds at many places children met together to greet her,—boys and girls, sons and daughters of the cowherds such as krishna loved in Brindaban. Mira meets the children. Mira feels the spiritual magnetism of children. Mira gazes at their faces and drinks in their sincerity, simplicity, spirituality, even as they drink in the love and longing of Mira's heart. Mira rejoices to see the love-lit faces of children. She looks at them. And she says:- "What a picture! A picture of trust and faith are these little ones! A picture of *bhakti*!"

Yes,-children know nothing of your "big" things,- your business, your earthly transactions. One rich treasure the little ones have:

they have not lost the meaning of holy things. And, looking at Mira, they cry:-"Mother! bless thy children!"

They join her in her singing. And the birds make a consecrated chorus: they sing the song of angels and seraphims. Mira sees that in the faces of the little ones is veiled the Face of Krishna. On more than one occasion, Mira holds out her hand,-the little, white hand of one who, indeed, was fair as she was pure,-the hand of a queen among women. And holding out her hand she says:-"Give me what you will!" A queen begging of these poor children and saying:-"Give me what you will!"

And they bring her rice and curds and a vegetable to eat. And she accepts it all with love and gratitude in her heart. The, looking at them, Mira says with teartouched eyes:-"My little ones! how shall I bless you? You have given me richly of the love of your hearts!"

Mira's heart is filled with hunger and thirst for krishna's love. Mira is *bhakti*-filled, *bhakti*-intoxicated. So were Sahajo Bai, and Daya Bai- the two sisters who sang lyric songs and who came many years after Mira had passed away. So, in another country, beyond the borders of India, in Basra, sang the *bhakti*-filled love intoxicated Rabia, the mystic-singer of Islam. So have sung, too, other singers of the Lord in other lands, in other ages. In every one of them, has sung a song, which hath been a holy descent from the Eternal on the human heart. And the cry of every one of these lyric singers of love hath been:-"OThou, the Ravisher of the heart! O Thou, the Joy of life!"

As gold burnt in fire is purified, so is Mira's soul purified in the fire of love and longing for her Lord. This purification comes after renunciation (1) of earthly honours, and (2) of creaturely affection. Renunciation of this kind is accompanied by an intense longing, often referred to as "burning of the heart."

In a suggestive, little story, we read of a scholar who has longed for spiritual life for a number of years and who cries out:-"O Lord!show me a man who would teach me the Truth!"

And there comes to the scholar a Voice, saying:-"Go to yon shrine of worship and you will find a man who will show you the way of blessedness."

And going there, the scholar finds a man, who is poor, whose feet are torn and covered with dust and dirt and whose clothes are soiled. Of him the scholar asks:- "Whence are you?"

The answer given is:-"From God."

Of him the question is asked again:- "Where did you find God?"

The poor man says:- "I found Him in detachment: I found the Lord of all in renouncing *moha,* attachment. "

Mira, renouncing all *moha,* moves on, from place to place. After this "renunciation," comes darkness, suffering, pain. And after suffering and pain, her life is enriched with that *concentration* which deepens into devotion,-*bhakti* of the highest type for the Lord.

To Mira, Krishna now is become the Lamp of her life. Krishna, too, becomes her Way, the Path which she treads, travelling on and on. and every step she treads is filled with spiritual anguish. Krishna hath captivated her: Krishna hath wounded her! Steep is the Ascent of Love and steep is the Path of Mira's quest.

She moves on! She sings on! Her songs are in brijabhasha or Gujerati or Hindi of Northern India They are penetrated with the power of spiritual music. It is the music of the Great Heart vibrating to the pilgrim's heart.

If the earlier stage is that of "burning love," the next stage is that of "songful love," love filled with "joy,"- which the *rishi* of the *Upanishad* refers to as *ananda* (joy). From *ananda,* the *rishi* says, hath flowed the universe: and to *ananda* will return all that is! Mira's sorrow, her longing, her yearning, every aspiration of her heart is now turned into a song of joy. Listen to one of her songs at this stage:-

Inebriate with love am I:
And no one knows of the love
Born within me.
Sing thou, my heart!
Sing thou of the Lotus-feet
Of the Ageless One!
Behold! All that is on earth below

And in the skies above
And between the earth and sky
Will pass away!
So be not vain
Of thy body and thy brain!
Of dust are they:
To dust will they return!
O wanderer! Wander no more1
Thy way is not to wander thus!
Thy way is still to sing the Name
In love at the Lotus-feet!

Mira now has entered into a new realisation. She sees her Beloved everywhere. She feels the Universal Life, the Life Divine. She looks around: she feels that full of Krishna are all the streets and all the market-places of men. She sees the world is full of God. She has held her senses in check and now transcends them. She has passed through the painful process of purification and has now enriched her life with devotion to the Lord and fellowship with the poor and suffering ones in whom she sees the *rupas*, the Images of her Lord. The creatures by themselves, she feels, are nothing."The Friend,"she says, "is every thing."

Mira has passed through "experience" of anguish to the "conquest"of the senses. She has attained to "*yoga*," "union" in holiness. And becoming holy, she well may spend herself not only in singing of the Lord, but in service of the Eternal, who incarnates Himself in the poor and the lowly.

Mira now breathes out but one simple prayer:-"O Krishna! O Beloved!" She needs not many words to open out her heart to her Lord, Krishna, the Ancient, krishna, the Unborn, krishna, the Purest of the pure Krishna, the Holy of holies, Krishna, the Stainless Krishna, the Prince of peace, Krishna, the Dweller in silence, Krishna, the Light of Lights,-Krishna is now seen by her to be the Life of her life. "I live not for me," she feels; "Krishna liveth in me!" The sun, the moon and stars are Krishna-fragments. And Krishna is in the sea and the rocks, in the trees and the flowers. The life of each individual is hidden in Him: and He liveth in each.

Each blade of grass now speaks to Mira,sings to her:-

"Krishna! My Krishna!
I know none other but Thee!

Krishna's Name Shines in every star. To her, Krishna is in the ant, in dung, in dust, in *maya*, as Krishna, too, is in the pure, the sintly, the holy, In every flower and wave is He: in every bird and form of beauty is He. In the sweetness of spring is He. And is He not the spark at the centre of every soul?

Mira has, after passing through a great agony of separation, broken at last the spell of *samsura*, the glamour of the world and its activities.

Mira's joy passes into what is deeper than "joy," passes into silence,-the silence of the mystic who utters not a word but gazes at Krishna, as Krishna in silence gazes at him. Mira, with tear-touched eyes, now looks on every creature as a *theophany* a *rupa*, a form, an image of Eternal Krishna.

Gone is now the illusion of separateness. Listen to one of Mira's songs in this connection:-

Forget not this, O man!
This human birth is thine,-
A gift from the Blessed One!
But this happens not again and again.
This body is a gift to thee from God
That thou mayst in wisdom grow
And sing in thy heart the Name!
And know this, too, O man!
Thou wilt not know the Name
Without the Guru's grace!
Without the Guru thou wilt go athirst.
But with the Guru's aid
A blind man, too, can drink
The nectar of the Name.

So have I found the Lord:
And I sing of Govinda, the Gracious One!

And so with faith in Him
I have entered into illumination
And the ecstasy of bliss!

What a thrill in these words of Mira! She hath attained, at last! She sings:-

Let my garment be dipped
In colours of the sunset!
Red is my heart
Dyed deep in colour
Of my Lover's love!
So crimson-red let my garment be!
For I go as a bride
To the bowers of the Beloved!
I go to greet Him!
I go to sing to Him my Song,-
The Song of Adoration and Love!

Brindaban-Leela

Brindaban, at last! Significant is the word, "Vrindavan," Vrinda is the sacred basil (*tulsi*) tree, and "bana" means "forest." Brindaban is the home of the sacred *tulsi* tree. Situated on the right bank of the river Jamuna, in the Mathura District, Brindaban is dear to every lover of Krishna. There Krishna played on the flute and threw the spell of his pure, divine love on all who saw Him and heard Him. And there a thousand temples stand dedicated to "Govinda Deva,"-to Krishna, the Guardian of cows and the cattle. Krishna is, in Brindaban, remembered as the *Deva*, the Divine Guardian and Servant of the cow and the cattle.

Mira has put on the *geruae* cloth. Mira has crossed forests and mountains. Mira has washed herself in the waters of sacred rivers. Mira has touched the dust of many Krishna-shrines on the way.

At Brindaban, there lives a great *bhakta* of Sri Chaitanya Mahaprabhu whose name is Jiv Goswami. Mira is anxious to have his *darshana*: and, standing at the Temple-gate, Mira sends a request to be permitted to see the Goswami.

He sends a word: "I never meet women!"

Mira sends an answer in the following words:- "O great one! I thought Gridhara, Sri Krishna, was the only *Purusha* (male) in Brindaban: and I thought everybody else was a woman in Brindaban. But now I know that Krishna has a compeer, that there is a second Krishna in Brindaban!"

Jiv Goswami is struck with Mira's answer. It goes right into his heart. He realises that Mira is no ordinary singer of Krishna. Mira, he understands, is a supreme *bhakta.* What Mira means is:-"I regard Krishna alone as the *Purusha*(male):I see all others as *sakhis* (females)."

And Jiv goswami quits his seat, quickly opens the gate of the Temple and, in great love, meets Mira.

With what love is Mira greeted by the people in Brindaban, as she moves along, crossing street after street! They come out of their houses and bow down to her in reverence. They gaze at her face and listen to the one word she utters again and again:- "Govinda! Govinda! Govinda!" In the simplest language, which is the language of love, she teaches them the great lesson of *bhakti,* the supreme lesson of self-surrender.

"Blessed is Mira," they say; "her touch sanctifies the soil made sacred by krishna's contact and communion, in the long ago." some say:-"Her songs bring back to us the ancient memory of *rasa-lila.*" Some say:- "When she dances in ecstasy, we see Krishna again." Some say:- "We feel that Shyama is nigh to us as we sit at her feet and as we gaze at her holy face rapt in meditation." Some say:- "Wonderful is she! Once a queen, she comes to us today in the garb of a beggar,-a wanderer in the streets of Brindaban. Blessed, blessed be Mira!

Little ones, the children of cowherds, come running to her and touch her feet and say:-"O Blessed One! here is milk for thee. Drink and bless us!" Not a few, bowing to her in reverence, say:- "O Holy One! sing again to us the ancient, forgotten song of the *gopis* of Brija." And Mira gently, in deep humility, sings her one-word song:-"Govinda! Govinda! Gridhari! Gridhara Nagara!" She sings, then weeps, then laughs, then falls down unconscious! Does she swoon or does she rest in the Holy Lap of her Beloved?

Every day of her stay at Bridaban is a day of joy in Krishna's adoration, a day of *kirtan* before the Image of Shyama. And everyday, she looks at the trees of Brindaban, and to every tree and every leaf and every flower.she says:-"Blessed art thou! Thou and I have been together, birth after birth!"

Mira rejoices in the thought that Krishna did, in the long ago, cast His holy glance on every lane in Brindaban. Putting on her feet the little bells and taking in her hands *kartala* she sings as one who is love-intoxi-cated. She calls herself *prema-devani*(love-intoxi-cated). With tear-filled eyes, she does *arati* (worship) to Krishna,-tears flowing from her eyes profusely. And even when her eyes are shut, she sees the Beloved and cries, again and again:- "My Master!" Mira sees Krishna everywhere. Every flower and every tree, every leaf and every stone is Krishna's. She, too, is His! For her *samsara* (the world) has vanished in the one vision of Krishna. Yes,-the inner door of her heart is opened and she is filled with interior illumination. "Light! Light!" she cries, again and again. In a beautiful, little song, she sings thus:-

In mine eyes
And in the heart within me
Thou art!
Beloved, Thou art!
And to Thee I come
Radiant in Thy colour divine!

And again:-

Krishna! O Krishna!
Behold!, The world is all asleep:
I keep awake!
In my heart is yearning
For Thee, alone for Thee!
I sit and weave
A garland of tears:

I count the stars:
And lo! the night is gone!
Beloved, meet me!
O meet me!
No more separation!
Krishna, my Life!
Krishna, my Communion!
Krishna, my Heaven!
Krishna, my All!

Thus doth Mira sing of Shyama. And singing of Him, she falls unconscious, she goes into ecstasy, again and again. Then, waking up, she cries out:-"Krishna! Krishna!"

In her *kirtan* and aspiration, in her wanderings from *kunja* (bower) to *kunja* in Brindaban, in the tears she sheds, in the little songs she sings, Mira adores Krishna as the Truth of her life.

Again and again, she feels happy in the thought that she has known Krishna, having renounced all arguments, controversies, discussions, debates. Krishna is to her a Reality, an immediate perception. And Krishna's knowledge is to her a revelation of God.

The City Of Many Gates

After a brief stay, Mira leaves Brindaban. Some say she goes back to her village, Merta, and stays there for a short time. From Merta she comes to Dwarka.

On the sea-shore, in Kathiawar, did krishna build Dwarka, "Dvara-vati," "the City of many gates," in the long ago. And Krishna taught that "there be many gates to God, and by whatever gate My *bhaktas* come with love to worship Me, on that gate stand I to greet them."

With the dawn doth Mira see Dwarka, the Ever-blessed! It shineth in her eyes. Dim streets she sees afar. Each tree and leaf, each flower and wave doth know her. For Krishna, her Beloved, once did dwell in Dwarka and bless its birds and consecrated cows and gardens fair, and on the sea-shore did Krishna play on His magic flute, even as it rained day by day and night after night.

With love and reverence in her heart doth Mira stand on the sea-shore, rapt, intoxicate. And Mira gazes at the waves, then bursts into song after song. Before her and all around,-here, there, everywhere,-she sees Krishna, Krishna!

With what longing in her heart singeth Mira of her Beloved:-

I love Thee, Shyama!
I love Thee more than life!
My strength, my solace and my bliss
In Thee alone I find.-
In Thee and Thy Holy Name.-
My sweetest one!
When all is dark
Thy Name awakes in me a Light!
It burneth as a Flame
In my heart: day and night
It shines before me
As a Torch of Light.
Beautiful and bright!

Mira spends her time in the Sri Ranchore Temple, sacred to Sri Krishna. There she does *kirtan* to the glory of her Lord. A number of devout ladies join her. With these she builds a little Group of Devotees, her *bhakta-mandali.*

A tradition has it that, one day, Rana Vikramajit comes secretly from Chitor to meet her in Dwarka and implores her to return to Chitor, saying:-"Since the day you left the palace, Chitor has had to face many difficulties." And the people tell me:-"Our sufferings are due to the treatment given to Mira." I come to ask you to forgive me. "Bless me and return with me to Chitor!"

Mira repeatedly requests to be excused. The Rana returns alone, but sends a number of Brahmins to persuade her to come back to Chitor. They are wonderstruck at what they see. Mira is absorbed in her *kirtan*!

The Brahmins sit at her door, saying:-"O Holy One! We cannot go without you. Nor can we eat any thing, until you come back with us to Chitor!"

Mira feels it is a sin to let the Brahmins stay and starve. She says to them:-"Do let me have a little time; and let me go to the Temple to take leave of my Beloved and get His blessings before I go back with you to Chitor."

It is dusk: vanished is the warmth of daylight. Mira enters the Temple alone. In silence she stands before the Image of her Lord,-the Beloved. "More to me than life," she says, "art Thou, Beloved! In mine eyes and in my heart Thou art! Thou art!" And she sings:-

The Bread of my soul art Thou!
The Strength of my heart art Thou!
The Treasure of my life art Thou!
Methinks, I hear Thy Voice.
I hear the sound of Thy Flute.

Sometimes I see Thee
Coming quick from a grove.
Beautiful and bright!
And over Thee I see
A touch of Fire,
A Flame of Beauty!
And from the Flame doth come
A Voice: but I understand it not.
And I sob and cry:-
'O meet me, Master!'
No more separation!

Sometimes I see,
When all is dark,
That in the Heart within
Doth shine a Light, Thy Light!
And then I cry:-
'I have seen
What I have seen!'
And again I cry:-
'Holy! Holy! Holy!
The Holy one have I seen!'

And a Voice I hear again:
It speaketh to my heart:-
'Open to Me.
For I come quickly!'
I open! But Thou art gone!

And Mira weeps. O, the tears! And Mira sings again:-

In Thee, Beloved, is Light:
And the Light doth shine
In darkness of the world,
And the world knows it not!
O Light! Eternal Light!
With a million eyes dost Thou
Fill all worlds, all stars and suns.
With a mercy immeasurable
Dost Thou shine on me,-
A pilgrim through endless space
To Thy Holy Shrine!

Then, with tear-touched eyes, doth Mira sing again:-

Beloved!
Thy Light doth shine
On herb and grass,
On flower and fruit,
On drops of dew,
On beauty of the clouds,
On running streams,
On falling rains.
On winds and wheeling fires,
On thorns and roses soft,
On every birth
And every silence
Of night and sleep!

Then in utter devotion, she sings again:-

O come Thou quick!
For, lo! I faint for Thee!

Beloved!
Come! Come! Come!
O Lights of lights!

Mira is adoring her Beloved within closed doors. The Temple-room is fragrant with the fragrance of Him who is the Purest of the pure. Mira is dancing in the presence of her Beloved.

Again and again, she exclaims:-"OThou, the Treasure of my heart! O Thou, the Breath of my breath!"

It is evening. Mira is doing *arati* to her Lord.

The evening hours slip, one by one, into the hour of the midnight.

Then Mira holds out her arms to embrace Krishna's Image. And the story has it that the Image stretches forth Its arms to greet her!

Mira falls down unconscious. A stream of tears is flowing from her eyes. Mira is mingled with her Beloved,"Madhava." No separation now! Mira is become one with the Holy One who is in All!

And the Temple is filled with a trange, mysterious light such as seldom was on earth or sea.

Rishi Dayanand : A Spiritual Athlete

In Quest

THE OTHER NIGHT. I looked at the stars and I said:—"These stars also looked upon the India of the long ago." Then, in anguish of the heart, I asked:- "But how many remember that India? How many remember her ancient message:-"The Eternal is one and hath no caste'?"

This message became elquent in the lives of a few great Indians in the last century. Each one of them was a witness to India's vision through the ages. Eath one was a herald of the future Each one was a torch-bearer. One such was Rishi Dayanand, the founder of the Arya Samaj.

He will, I believe, challenge attention in the coming days. His life and message have, I submit, a world-value.

"The development of a soul!" says Browning; "little else is worth study." And the story of the development of Dayanand's soul has a strange fascination for me.

His life falls into five broad divisions:-

1. Period of boyhood and youth: 1824-1845;
2. Period of quest: 1846-1860;
3. Period of discipleship: 1860-1863;
4. Period of "retreat": 1863;
5. Period of preaching and organisation upto 1883.

He is born, in 1824 , in Tanakara,-a village in the Morvi State in Kathiawar. His father is a rich banker named Ambashankar. He does not know that his son is destined to become a shankar of modern India in Sanskrit scholarship and dialectics. Dayanand's like Shankar's, was an exploring mind. Ambashankar is not only a banker but, also, a *zemindar* and a *jamadar*, i.e. a town revenue collector and magistrate. And he worships Shiva and Lakshmi. So does the son then named Mulshankar. He delights in *kathas* of Shiva.

In 1838, on the Shivratri night, he follows his father to the Shiva temple, keeps fast, wakes up the whole night, and sees a mouse running over the Shiva-image and eating the food offered to God. The Divine Spirit touches the soul in diverse ways. And Mulshankar hears the Atman's voice while still a boy of fourteen. It speaks to him on this memorable Shivratri night. The action of the mouse taking liberties with the God awakens, in Mulshankar's mind, a questioning which, in due course, develops into quest. The boy asks himself:-"Can this image be the Lord of the universe?"

The path of truth is the path of questions and answers. Many a man had seen an apple fall. It was Newton who saw and asked:- "why falls an apple to the ground?" And after patient search there came to him the answer,-the law of gravitation. Newton became a *rishi* of science. Many had been to the temple to offer devotions to Shiva. It was Dayanand who, seeing a mouse running over the image, asked:-"Can this image be the Supreme Being, the real Lord of Life?"

Mulshankar's father, unable to wake up long, has fallen asleep. Other worshippers, too, are asleep.- outside the shrine. Alone Mulshankar keeps awake. Thoughts upon thoughts crowd in upon his mind. Can this image be the Mahadeva, the great God of the universe? Dayanand writes in his "Autobiography":-

Unable to resist such thoughts any longer. I roused my father, abruptly asking him to enlighten me, to tell me whether this emblem of Shiva in the temple was identical with the Mahadeva. the great God of the Scriptures.

"Why do you ask?" questioned my father.

"Because." I answered. "I feel it impossible to reconcile the idea of an omnipotent living God with this idol which allows the mice to move over his body and thus suffers his image to be polluted without the slightest, protest."

Mulshankar has heard the call, and he must go in search of the Great Solution, must wander in quest of the One God beyond all Gods. He must renounce his parents and home. He cannot renounce Truth.

Some years pass. The *Atman's* voice speaks to him, again, through the death of his sister-a girl of fourteen. "It was my first bereavement," writes Dayanand, "and the shock my heart received was great I stood like one petrified and plunged in profound reverie."

What must one do to escape impermanence, to meet, the challenge of death, to enter into immortality? Such questions agitate the mind of Mulshankar. He is only eighteen years of age. But he has begun to see the "instability of life." he understands that impermanent are the lives of men, that he, too, must face death one day, and that none there is who will save from the "tyrant-clutches" of death. On whom then may he rely for salvation?

Soon after, his uncle dies,-"a very learned man," writes Dayanand, "and full of divine qualities, one who had shown for me the greatest tenderness and whose favourite I had been from my birth,-his death leaving me in a state of utter dejection and with a still profounder conviction that there was nothing stable in this world, nothing worth living for or caring for in a worldly life."

Mulshankar is now twenty years of age. He longs for Knowledge. He asks his father to send him to Kasi (Banaras), the great seat of Hindu culture. His mother, with a woman's intuition , sees that her son wishes to go to kasi in order to escape marriage. "Men of knowledge," she says. "seldom wish to marry. And there will be obstacles in your marriage if you go to Kasi." Then Mulshankar asks for leave to study at the feet of a Brahmin in a neighbouring village. To this Brahmin, Mulshankar opens out his heart saying how repulsive seems to him the idea of marriage. The Brahmin reports the matter to Mulshankar's father who now makes hurried preparations for his son's marriage.

Mulshankar is twenty-two years of age. already the *Atman's* "wireless" is working within him. Truth is calling him, as truth ever does, to wilderness. He sets his face against attractions of the world. He resolves, to quote his words, "to place an eternal barrier between myself and marriage."

He secretly leaves his rich father's house in quest of the soul's Homeland. It is the year 1846. Wealth he spurns, for he seeks wisdom. *Bhoga* (sense-gratification) he shuns, for he wants *yoga* (union with the Divine Spirit). His father, with a party of sepoys, pursues his son and catches him at Siddpur in a Shiva temple. Dayanand writes:-

My father had come down to Siddpur with his sepoys, traced me step by step in the *mela* (religious gathering), learning something of me wherever I had sat among the learned *pundits* and, finally, one fine morning, appeared suddenly before me. His wrath was terrible to behold. He reproached me violently and accused me of bringing eternal disgrace upon my family. As soon as I met his glance, I knew well it was no use trying to resist him. I suddenly made up my mind how to act. I fell at his feet with folded hands and, in supplicating tones, tried to appease his anger. I said:- "I was myself feeling miserable here and was just on the point of returning home when you, father! have providentially arrived. I am willing now to follow you home again."

This Dayanand confesses; was not true. He had not thought of returning home: he was not willing to return home. "My determination," Dayanand writes, "was as firm as his own. I was bent on my purpose and closely watched for an oportunity to escape again."

Fear is the mother of untruth. Therefore did the Sage Manu declare that you must neither fear others nor make others fear you. Dayanand tells us truthfully that he spoke untruth to his father. His father, in a fit of rage, tears his son's yellow robe to pieces. violently removes from his hands the *tumba* (the hermit's bowl), calls him a "matricide," and hands him over to his "sepoys" who are asked to watch him, day and night. But Dayanand makes good his escape again at three in the morning, when the "sepoy" in charge of him is asleep.

The path of truth is paved with tragedy and tears. For fifteen long years he wanders in quest. He reaches Ahmedabad. He proceeds to Baroda. He comes under the influence of Brahmanand,- a Vedantist. He repairs to the banks of the Narbada. There he meets learned *sanyasins*. He meets Swami Paramanand Saraswati of Sringaree Math of Shankaracharya in the South. This Swami, profoundly versed in Vedantic philosophy, initiates him into *sanyasa*, delivers to him a *danda* (symbol of initiation), and gives him the name destined to endure in the history of modern India. Mulshankar is named Dayanand Saraswati.

It is a moving story this,-of Dayanand still moving from place to place in search of Truth. In his wanderings, he meets a rich *mahant* (abbot) who offers him the *mahantship* (headship) of a monastery. Dayanand spurns the offer and says:-"I have renounced everything to have Knowledge, *mukti*." Marriage and money are not for him. "To take up the task of a New Reformation is my real mission," he says in his "Autobiography."

Thinking of Dayanand, I recall the life of Saint Anthony. Born of wealthy parents, he hears one day the word of Christ:-"Go and sell all thou hast!" Anthony feels the words are addressed to him. He renounces the world and goes out to begin a new life of *tapasya*. Dayanand , too, renounces the world and goes out,-a pilgrim in quest. Who is his father and who is his mother? The GreatOne whose worship is the service of Truth. And where does Dayanand seek his home? In the hearts of all in every land who would serve God and re-build the Aryan race.

The Blind Monk Of Mathura

Why is Dayanand's life a benediction and an inspiration to his race? One truth he realises at an early age:- "I belong to Truth." And in search of Truth he wanders from place to place. His courage does not fail him. His faith is strong :- "Lead, Kindly Light!"

He goes to Ahmedabad to meet some *yogis*. He passes on to Mount Abu. He crosses over to Srinagar and stays for sometime at the Kedar Ghat, looking for some great *yogis* but finding none. No difficulties daunt this young *sanyasi* destined to be a soldier of Truth.

In 1860, Dayanand comes to Mathura and there meets a Blind Monk. Has he not been waiting all these years for this Man of

Destiny? Would India have known of Rishi Dayanand if he had not met Maharishi Virajanand? Dayanand remembers his Guru, again and again, in his writings. At the close of each chapter of his "Veda Bhasha," Dayanand writes:-"The commentary in this chapter is written by Dayanand,-a disciple of Swami Virajanand."

Virajanand was a son of Pandit Narain Datta Bhardwaj. At the age of five, the boy had an attack of smallpox and became blind. He became an orphan at the age of fifteen. He consecrated his life to study and meditation. At eighteen, he was initiated into *sanyasa* by Swami Purananand and was named Virajanand. This Blind Monk developed into a profound Vedic scholar. Not without reason was he popularly known as "Pragna Chakku," "the Wise-eyed one."

The Prince of Alwar heard Virajanand recite hymns of Sri Shankaracharya and, being greatly moved, invited him to Alwar. The Monk agreed on the one condition that the Prince would read the Scriptures with him for three hours every day. "But if any day you do not read with me three hours," the Monk added. "I shall leave you and your State." The Prince attended to the Sage with all possible care. One day, the Prince, attracted to a pleasure-party, absented himself from the Swami's class. When next the Prince met Virajanand,the latter expressed his resolve to leave the State, saying:-"You, Prince, have broken your promise, but I cannot." Virajanand left Alwar for Bharatpur. After sometime he came to mathura and started a Sanskrit *pathshala* (school).

At the door of this *bal brahmachari* and *tapasvi* knocks, one day, another bal brahmachari and tapasvi. The door is closed. A voice from within asks:- "Who are you?"

"A sanyasi *?"*

"What is your name?"

"Dayanand Saraswati."

The door is opened. Virajanand accepts Dayanand as his pupil and disciple. With what love and reverence Dayanand serves his Guru, fetching water from the stream for his morning bath, sweeping the courtyard of his house, and gladly accepting the most rigorous discipline! Even the harsh epithets sometimes used by Virajanand are welcomed by Dayanand as the Guru's "garlands." Long after, Dayanand would show with pride the scars of wounds on his body caused by the stout *lathi* (stick) of Virajanand and say:- "Behold the scars on my body: they are the marks of my Guru's love! " And when Dayanand learnt of his master's death, he exclaimed:-"Today the sun of Sanskrit scholarship is set."

At the feet of this Blind Monk of Mathura,- a profound Vedic scholar,- Dayanand studies the *Rishi-Krita*' Granthas,-the Books written by rishis in the days of India's spiritual and intellectual greatness. Dayanand drinks deep of Vedic wisdom at the feet of his Guru. Then Dayanand feels it is high time for him to go. His Guru gives him blessings and a great message:-

> Go thou, my child, and spread the message!
> There is ignorance in the land:
> The people know not the right from wrong.
> They quarrel about castes and creeds
> And know not the Vedas.
> Go thou and give the great message
> Of One God and Vedic Wisdom.

It is time for Dayanand to return to the world to give his message, to utter aloud the Answer that has come to him after years of search and *sadhana*:- "He is the One Eternal self, *Sat Chit Ananda* and in serving Him is your salvation!"

A remarkable figure, as you picture Dayanand coming out of his seclusion and standing before others with his message. Only a loin-cloth on his body! But the "priests" are filled with fear at his approach. he knows no fear. In his heart is the Vedic aspiration: "May I attain to Light with fearlessness!

For twenty years. from 1863 to 1883, he travels all over the country, holding in his hands the torch of Aryan Wisdom. He preaches a message of race-regeneration. He pleads for worship of One God. for social reform and for cow-protection.

At Agra, Gwalior, Jaipur, Kasi, Ajmer, Bombay, Poona, Calcutta, Patna, Jodhpur,-wherever he goes, he takes with him the message of the Aryan Ideal of which the deepest note is Unity, and the Aryan civilisation of which the symbol is the "Cow." His lectures everywhere arrest attention: they are a challenge at once to Hindu ecclesiasticism, and Western externalism.

His visit to Calcutta is significant. He comes in contact there with Sri Keshub Chandra Sen, one of the great mystics of his century. The two become friends the very first day they meet. There is a law by which soul gravitates to soul: the truly great ones recognise one another at a glance.

On the very first occasion, Keshub asks Dayanand:-

"Have you seen Keshub Chandra Sen?"

After exchanging a few words, Dayanand says:- "You are Keshub Chandra Sen!"

After this, the two meet each other almost daily and talk for hours together, Great souls are linked, one with the other, by a pre-established harmony. Alas! it is often the disciples who quarrel! Keshub arranges the very first lecture of dayanand. Keshub. too, suggests to Dayanand to speak in Hindi Dayanand returns from Calcutta with the idea of founding a Samaj to preach the Vedic Ideal. He starts the first Arya Samaj in Bombay, in the year 1875.

I am not competent to speak of the work the Arya Samaj has done. I regard it as a wonderful work. Two of its ten principles are:- (1) to do good to the world by improving the physical, intellectual, moral, social and spiritual conditions of mankind; (2) to diffuse Knowledge and dispel ignorance.

Be it said to the credit of the Arya Samaj, it has done fine work in education and social service. The Samaj has centres in Burma, British Africa and the Fiji Islands besides many branches in India. It has schools and orphanages. It has colleges and *gurukulas.* It has worked for female education and temperance. It has brought back many of the "untouchables" to the Hindu fold.

Rishi Dayanand, I humbly submit, belongs not to the Arya Samaj alone. He belonges to India. He belongs to the world. Someone defined genius as a flower of culture. Dayanand was a flower of Aryan culture. The very essence of this culture is spiritual oneness of Humanity. Dayanand believed neither in caste nor sect. He believed in Brotherhood. In his heart sang the Vedic voice:-"Come, speak sweetly one to the other! I make you one-willed and one-minded!"

A man of a superior caste is about to turn a butcher out of a meeting which Dayanand is addressing. He rebukes the rich man's pride in significant words:- "For butchers is meant my message." A barber offers him coarse bread. Dayanand eats it joyfully. A dancing-girl sees him in meditation and is moved to offer him her gold ornaments. He says he does not want them. and he asks her to go and sin no more.

A retired Government servant meets him. The Swami says to him:- "You are a Brahmin. Your ancestors were regarded as teachers and inspirers. They spent their lives in the service of mankind. You must follow in their footsteps. Take a vow of service. and go and work among the *bhils* (a class of untouchables)."

A poor old woman meets him on the way. She is clothed in rags. she says:- "I have none to look after me. God will bless you: give me food." Tears stand in his eyes: and he says to his companions:- "There was a time when Bharat was full of gold. There was such abundance that orphans and the hungry could not be found: but today poverty is so great that this woman begs of a man who is a beggar himself!" Then he asks his companion to give food to the lady.

In his heart is such tender love for the poor and the outcasts! He leaves his father's weatlth and happy home to join the brotherhood of the poor. He trains himself in the school of hardness. He fasts for several days. He sleeps on the gound, making bricks his pillow. For years he wanders from place to place with only a strip of cloth on his body. He prefers the poor man's cottage to the rajah's palace. He presses the outcast and lowly to his heart.

A man of what is called a "low caste" brings him rice and curry to eat. Dayanand accepts the gift of love. A Brahmin who is present says to Dayanand:-"You are polluted, for you have eaten the meals brought by this man."

Dayanand says:- "Food may be polluted in two ways,- either when it is procured by force causing pain to another or when it is mixed with a dirty thing. But here is a poor man earning his bread with the sweat of his brow. His food is the best."

Dayanand proclaims the "One without a caste," and he calls to his Samaj orphans and outcasts, widows and the famine-stricken, the poor and the lowly of all castes, all communities.

In the heart of Rishi Dayanand was immense love for the poor and downtrodden. And without such love you may not hope to build a new nation. Meetings and speeches will not help you. Knowledge itself without *tapasya* and love is empty. Young men! they are waiting for you,-the peasants. the village-folk, the poor and the lowly, In thousands and tens of thousands they wait for you. Go to them with *kathas* and *Kirtans* and Vedic hymns and the message of the heroes of Indian history. Go to them and build in their minds and hearts a new India.

Rishi Dayanand's achievements: not many of his countrymen are aware of them. We live, alas! in forgetfulness. He kindled a new nation-consciousness. He vindicated Aryan civilisation. He re-proclaimed the Vedic religion. And the secret of it is, to my mind, expressed in the Vedic prayer:-"May life be strengthened through sacrifice!"

Was not Rishi Dayanand's life one of sacrifice? Of an ancient Greek thinker they asked what was the source and the secret of his wisdom. "i wandered," he said, "to Italy, to Greece, to Africa. At last, I came to India. And there I saw a naked man. To him God was the Great Reality. And his was a life of daily sacrifice. This man, the Indian, was truly wise."

May not similar words be spoken of Rishi Dayanand? This *sanyasi* this *fakir*, rich in knowledge, rejoicing in poverty, wandering from place to place, almost naked,wandering to give his message to a people forgetful of their ancient heritage,-Rishi Dayanand rejoiced in God as the Great Reality. "This man. the Indian, was truly wise." And his was a life of sacrifice.

A Spiritual Athlete

Why do I ask young men to study the life of Dayanand? He showed in his life and teaching his profound belief in the message of *shakti*. It is an integral *shakti* of body and mind and soul.

Dayanand was a man of *shakti.* This man in langoti had a strong body. "The servants of God," he writes in his "Ved Bhashya," "should realise that they must develop their physical powers." Both body and soul, he urges, should grow in strength, "For," he writes in the "*Satyarth Prakash,*" "if only mental powers and knowledge be developed but not physical strength, one man of great physical strength may vanquish hundreds of scholars. Let both mind and body be developed."

I believe that body-building is character-building, is nation-building. I believe in the spiritual value of physical culture. To young men eager for India's service. I say:- "Build up your bodies!"

Many are the stories told of the physical strength of Dayanand. He is on his way to Banaras. On account of the rains the roads are muddy. A cart is stuck in the mud. The cart-man, unable to pull it up, is beating the pullocks mercilessly. Dayanand goes to the rescue of the poor animals. Dayanand asks the driver not to beat the bullocks and, loosening their yoke, pulls up the cart out of the mud! On another occasion, he holds form behind a carriage to which a horse is yoked: the horse is unable to move! Verily, this *rishi* of modern India was an athlete. True spirituality is not soft sentimentalism. True spirituality is athletic.

This spiritual athlete of India, this man of *shakti* was fearless. He says:- "I fear none except the *Narayana Parmatman* (God)" One day, Dayanand is having a bath in the Ganges when a crocodile is seen near him. A man, seeing it, cries wildly:-"A crocodile! A crocodile!" Dayanand shows no sign of fear or agitation. Quietly, he says:- "When I have no wish to harm it, it will not harm me.

Some rowdy persons attack hims and his followers during a religious debate. He returns to his residence. The rowdies attack it. An attendant goes out to keep them quiet. They beat him badly. Dayanand learns of it and immediately goes out to his attendant's rescue. With a stick in hand, Dayanand shouts to the rowdies. They cannot overcome this man of *shakti* and they take to their heels!

He does not mince matters. This spiritual athlete speaks truth as he sees it in the midst of hostile crowds. Speaking to an audience in the presence of an Indian Prince, he says:- "He who being a Raja keeps a prostitute is himself of her caste." The Prince says:- "You have not spared me!" Dayanand's answer is: -"I speak truth, favouring none. This is my *dharma*."

He is sincere, even to bluntness. And this his soft critics have called his "intolerance." Dayanand is intolerant of what he regards as superstition and hypocrisy. He cannot barter conviction for convenience. He suffers but complains not. He suffers with the gladness of a hero.

Dayanand preaches a message of *shakti*. And India needs all possible strength at this time. India needs a message of *shakti*. It is the strong who save their nation. The world respects the strong. Goodness without strength is a poor spectacle. It is said in unity is strength. It may be said with equal truth that out of strength springs unity,- and freedom.

Be strong,-is the *mantra* for modern India. It is the *mantra* of the ancient *rishis*. In the Yajur Veda we read:-"Be thou strog in body and mind." Dayanand was imbued with the spirit of *shakti*. He made not apologies, but went about giving frankly, plainly, his great message. Critics called him "aggressive." Some abused him. Some pelted stones at him. But he challenged attention. He fought as a soldier of the Spirit. He went about to rouse his countrymen. They had long accepted their humiliating state in the name of *kismet* (fate). Dayanand called them to the destiny of a great future. How strong was his body! Many of our young men have weak bodies. Physical weakness means loss in manhood. It is the manly who achieve. Build up your bodies,- I say to the young.

The basis of body-building is *brahmacharya*. Young men today want *bhoga* (pleasures): and pleasure- hunting ends in weakness and disease. Control of the senses is the wisdom of the body.

Like his great guru Maharishi Virajanand, Dayanand was a *bal-brahmachari*. In *brahmacharya* was his strength.

Even as a boy of fourteen, he felt he was not meant for family life. To him came the call to be a builder of a family of the Nation. He could only be married to his mission. And he lived a life of strict rules, of *sadhana*.

One day, some ladies come to have his *darshan* and receive

religious instruction. And this is what he says to them:-"Get knowledge: don't make a *swami* or *fakir* your Guru. Your Gurus are your husbands. Serve them and be blessed." A wholesome advice which would save women from being deluded by many pharisees who, clothed in yellow robes, call themselves *swamis*!

Dayanand's life-long *brahmacharya* is wonderful. It reminds me of Shankar Acharya. Rightly says the Atharya Veda:- "He alone who observes *brahmacharya* becomes an *acharya* (teacher)."

With *brahmacharya*, Dayanand combines reverence for woman. Seeing a girl playing with children beneath a tree, he bows to her and says;-"She is *matra shakti*,-a symbol of the Mother-force." In everyone of the female sex, he sees symbol of the Mother. And it is his dream that some women, well-versed in the Vedas, may take the message of Aryan *rishis* to the women of India. A beautiful dream!In the day it is realised, some thing of the beauty of the ancient days will return, when India was blessed not only by *rishis* but, also, by *rishinis*,-ladies like Gargi and Maitreyi reckoned among sages and seers.

Brahmacharya I hold, must become the basis of new education, new social order, new politics, new nationalism, new civilisation. Ancient India's greatness was in this:-She believed profoundly in the power of *brahmacharya*. And *brahmacharya* means, in essence, the spirit of purity, simplicity and self-control. Without it no nation may advance.

Ancient India showed a beautiful spirit of *brahmacharya* and placed the fruits of her culture and civilisation at the feet of "Brahman" the Divine Spirit. Today, the nations have surrendered themselves to the senses. Two thousand years of christian era! Two thousand years of progress,-you say. This "progress" for many, many years has been a dance of death. This progress is *bhoga*. And civilisation's future is not in *bhoga* of the senses but in the *shakti* of a simple, spiritual life, in the power of the *Atman*, the Ideal.

One of the most moving pictures in world-literature is that of Bhishma's last scene in the Mahabharata. On a bed of arrows on the battle-field lies Bhishma. They bring him a comfortable pillow. He will not have it. "Sturdy soldiers will not have wool or cotton pillows." says this great *brahmachari.* Then he turns to Yuddhisthira and says;- "O king! listen to what I say about *brahmacharya.* There is nothing which cannot be achieved by the man who is a *brahmachari* from birth till death. By the practice of *brahmacharya*, many have attained to *brahma-loka* and have achieved, also, happiness here." "The *brahmachari*," we read in the Atharva Veda, "becomes a man par excellence, and shines upon the earth like a luminary."

Why is *brahmacharya* so highly praised in the scriptures? It is the secret of strength,-physical, mental and spiritual. Blood corpuscles of an organism that maintains well its vital electricity can battle better with septic or poisonous germs. The majority of men have yet to understand that purity or *brahmacharya* gives better health and healing than all the drugs of dispensaries can.

I believe, more and more people will, in the coming days, realise the biological value of *brahmacharya.* Out of it are strength and energy. And we know what enduring power Dayanand posessed. Something more,too, happens in the case of a life-long *brahmachari.* He develops wonderfully well his brain-power, his intuitions, and the power to influence and help others on the spiritual path.

Dayanand showed by precept and example that *brahmacharya* was quite different from dismal asceticism. "May my senses grow in perfection!" is the opening line in the Chandogya Upanishad. And the Vedas, with their repeated emphasis on *bala* (energy), inculcate a sublime doctrine of *shakti.* "Inspire our senses," says the Vedic sage. Rishi Dayanand taught that lacerations of the body could not lead Godward.

The senses are gates of knowledge. The doctrine of *brahmacharya* is a doctrine of *shakti* (vitality). It asks not that the body he maimed or neglected, but that it be trained, built up strong and pure. How else would it respond to higher vibrations and become a vehicle of spiritual life? "May my senses grow in perfection!" And there is not growth in perfection without purity. This truth is trampled upon by many of the gifted men of modern Europe,-men like the Italian poet, for instance, who says:-"Life is a kind of diffused sensuality."

This gospel of "diffused sensuality" is one extreme, as contempt for the senses is another. The senses are manifestations, instruments of the soul. Earth-life misses its purpose, if it despises matter. *Brahmacharya* demands that we keep our senses pure. If they are either overfed or starved, the result will be weakness, desease. lillusions. And Patanjali rightly urges that *yoga* is not to be taught ot those whose bodies are unsound. Religion is health.

Brahmacharya of the senses: and the first is *chakshu*, the eye. If only we realised how many sins are due to sight! A volume could be written on modern degradation through sight,-degradation due to dances, balls, theatres, cinemas, caricatures, sensational novels. Rishi Dayanand said to a Rais of Meerut:- "Don't see obscene plays nor attend *nautch* parties." They make the eyes impure.

Next comes *vak*. *Vak* is voice, utterance, sound, speech. It is that which makes inter-communion possible. It is the other side of thought. *Vak* must be purified. Therefore, utter what you believe to be true. Stifle not the utterance, the sound of your soul by conventions or customs. Speak out the truth,-but not in bitterness. Purify your *vak*, and your words will tell. Have you not noted how the *vak*, the speech, the word of a sincere man comes with a special meaning to the heart? Such *vak* is pure. So it touches the chord of the heart.

Then there is *brahmacharya* of *prana*. This, too, must be purified. *Prana* is life-breath, respiration. Often we control speech, but not the vibrations of *prana*: and we get bad dreams. So train yourself in the school of *brahmacharya* that your dream-state, your sub-conscious life may, also, be good and pure. "Repeat Om, day and night." said Rishi Dayanand . Men of prayer, indeed, can achieve much, becaause prayer, repetition of Om. purifies the *prana*.

Then comes *srotah*; it means hearing. To listen to *gossip* and idle talk is to break the brahmacharya of hearing. In books of the past great value is attached to hearing the Name of God.

Then there are the senses of touch and taste: they, too, should be purified. Spicy, stimulating foods and drinks are not for the *brahmachari*. Nor flesh diet. That meat-eating is essential to health is a view current among many young men in India. It is a view I have never understood. I rather think that to give up meat-eating is to improve one's health. Simple diet is the secret of health.

There is the *brahmacharya* of the *manas*, mind. How many observe it in actual life? Two things are essential. Keep out impure thoughts: and after you have grown in purity, don't have the pride of purity. The true *brahmachari* is humble: he knows his littleness in the presence of God, the Infinite.

There is the *brahmacharya* of the heart. Love is divine: but love is not passion. And *brahmacharya*, let it be remembered, is to be observed in all the four *asramas*, including the grahastha *asrama*. Marriage does not mean sexual license. Nor must we confound happiness with luxury, Its way seems pleasant, but it proves to be the way of death. One of the saddest things in modern India is the failure to recognise sanctity of the vital force,- the creative force in man.

Don't squander your forces, but develop your body and vigour and use it in the service of man. So may you be as the light, gay grass, humble yet strong. One by one, the senses must be purified and, also, the mind and the heart. And disciplining yourself in *brahmacharya*, you will be better prepared to assimilate the daily developing wonder of the world.

To practise *brahmacharya* is to co-operate with the creative forces of life. *Brahmacharya* is co-operation with the creative *shakti* of God. Today, alas! many waste the "seed" in sex-excesses. So the body and the brain become weak and the mind suffers in concentration.

Today there is lack of "discipline" in the life of our students in schools and colleges. When the *brahmacharya* vow is honoured again in the life of our students, a new strength will return to us, and with radiant bodies and eager minds and purified hearts and strong will-power, the youths of India will bloom again with the beauty of the Life Divine. Such youths will reveal the true character of bhahmacharya as "yagna" or "sacrifice" to the Eternal.

Today, the nation is losing her strength, more and more, in noises and tumults and shouts and pictureshows of a distracted life. A new love of silence and a new resolve to live the disciplined life of *brahmacharya* will give India the strength she needs to fulfil the dream of her Sages and go upon her great mission as a Healer of the nations and a Builder of a new civilisation of strength and sacrifice.

It is the pure who see the Beauty of nature and the Truth of life. Nietzsche said:- "Morality is the greatest enemy of life and all that is fundamental in life." In contrast to this was Rishi Dayanand's vision of the moral law, the law of *brahmacharya*, as the very soul of Aryan culture and Aryan civilisation. It was the vision of the ancient *rishi* who sang the truth that life at its highest was the Good bursting into forms of Beauty. Morality is at the heart of life. *Brahmacharya* touches the very roots of reality. And blessed are the pure, for they are the builers of their Race.

Arise ! Awake !

The city is asleep. Beneath the street light, I see a small band of singers. who are they, standing on the road in this early hour, when everything is hushed in holy silence? Who are they,- standing, singing a song?

Jai, Jai pitamai !
Parama Ananda Data !

That is the burden of their song. "Victory, victory to the Divine Father, the Giver of the Joy of Salvation!" How refreshing to hear it! There are so few, alas! in these days to sing of victory to God. And India, too, has learnt, more and more, to be modern and to forget her God.

Why do they sing victory to God this day? It is a day sacred to the memory of Rishi Dayanand. On his deathbed he was heard uttering the prayer:- "God's will be done! Om Shanti! Shanti! Shanti!" Methinks, there was in his heart an unuttered message:- "Not to one *samaj*, but to all my countrymen I commit the Aryan message. It is a message for the world."

And for delivering the Aryan message he suffered as the world's great ones have suffered in this worid of suffering and pain. Aristotle was banished: Galileo was imprisoned: Dayanand was persecuted. But he was dauntless.

From place to place, he moved with the mighty message:- "Awake! He found the people forgetful of their ancient heritage. He found scepticism among the educated, superstition among the masses and nationwide ignorance of the Aryan Ideal."

His soul rose in revolt against unreality in the name of religion. When at Hardwar, he had a flag over his house with the following words:- *"Pakhand khandanj pataka."* "The Flag is a call to destroy insincerity and untruth.' A symbol was this Flag of Dayanand's life. Dayanand was tremendously real.

"Sincerity,- a deep, great, genuine sincerity," Carlyle rightly said, "is the first characteristic of all men in any way heroic." There is the heroic in Dayanand . In his love of truth he spares neither prince nor priest. He suffers for his integrity, his love of reality. Many are annoyed with him: many call him an "atheist." Some even plot against his life.

The Maharaja of Udaipur invites him. Dayanand preaches against superstitions. The maharaja offers him *mahantship* of the Eklinga Temple, having a revenue of a lakh of rupees, if he (Dayanand) will only tune his teaching to orthodoxy. Dayanand has but one answer:he belongs to Truth.

From Udaipur he goes to Shahpura,-a small State. Here he receives an invitation from the maharaja of Jodhpur. Dayanand stays at Jodhpur for a few months and tries to infuse a new spirit in the Prince and the People. Soon, there are court-intrigues against him. He has offended a courtesan by reforming the Prince. One day, he catches cold and goes to bed without eating anything. But he drinks milk. Alas! there is poision in it. His cook, Jagannath, has been bribed. Dayanand forgives Jagannath and even gives him money to escape to Nepal. Dayanand's condition becomes worse everyday. He leaves Jodhpur for Mount Abu. The Prince with a sad heart walks on foot behing the Swami's palanquin for some distance. At Abu, he gets some relief. But his doctor presses him to go to Ajmer.

His condition becomes worse at Ajmer. It is the 30th of October. Dr. Newton and Hakim Pir Iman Ali are called in. Dayanand sends for two of his disciples in the afternoon. He asks them what they want. They say their one prayer is that he might improve. "It is only the body." Dayanand says; 'what better can it become?"

It is 5.30 p.m. He asks what the *paksha* and the date are. He looks up. He recites Vedic *mantras.* He offers prayers. He repeats *Gayatri.* He enters into *samadhi.* then opens his eyes and says:- "Merciful Lord! Thy will be done!"

He passes away! It is the sacred eve of the Deepavali, when Hindu India commemorates the ancient feast of lights. Sacred is the feast to Lakshmi,-the World-Mother. Sacred, too, is the day to Saraswati,-the Spirit of Wisdom. and, on the Deepavali Day, passed into the Brahma-loka a gracious son of Saraswati,-Dayanand,-he who worshipped the Eternal with what the Gita calls "sacrifice of Knowledge."

"Know thyself!" was the great message of Socrates. He believed in Truth and in the One Supreme Spirit; and he was condemned to death. He drank the cup of hemlock cheerfully and passed away in peace. "Know the Ancient Wisdom!" was the great message of Dayanand. He' too, believed in Truth and the One supreme Spirit. And he was given a slow poison. He forgave all. He passed away in peace.

There is a beautiful ancient *sutra* which says:- *"Uttishtha! jagrata!"* "Arise! Awake!" the Supreme inspiration of Dayanand's life is verily this,-its call to this ancient, long-suffering nation:-

Sons of the Sages of the East !
Ye have slumbered long.
It is time to awake
Uttishtha ! Jagrata !
Arise ! Awake !
Arise ! Awake !

Shri Ramakrishna Paramahansa: The Saint Of Dakshineswar

RAMAKRISHNA! THE NAME is music to my ears.

Ramakrishna! The name is, to me, a symbol which has its message at once for India and the West.

For India, too, is coming increasingly under the sweep of Western forces. In India so many, today, are thinking in terms of economics and of a civilisation of which the essence is industrialism. Out of industrialism are the issues of a materialistic outlook on life.

Alike in East and West, men are unhappy. All over the world, the state is being deified. Young men say, today, that communism is in their hearts,-not the teaching of the *rishis*, the seers and prophets of humanity. And Leningrad boasts of its Anti-religious Museum. The great cities of India talk of Marx and Lenin, forgetting the rich inheritance of the Gita and the Upanishads. An increasing number of Indian girls repeat the words of the young woman of the West, who said:- "We don't believe in God. There is no purpose to life: life has no meaning."

[1]

Over a century ago, was born, in a village in Bengal, one who revealed anew the wisdom of India. When they asked him, one day, to attend a religious meeting, welldressed in *dhoti* and *chaddar*, his reply was characteristic. He said:- "I can't be dressed like a Babu!" Ramakrishna always wished to be, not a "civilised" Babu, but a simple child of God, whom he loved to call his "Mother."

The wisdom of God, said Jesus, is revealed unto babes. Ramakrishna was, indeed, a babe, a child whose joy was in the presence of his Divine Mother. He and such as he may well be the hope of humanity. Out of hope will spring a new understanding of life; and out of understanding will blossom peace among the nations.

As the day of his birth-anniversary is drawing nigh, I hve meditated on this singular man and his simple teaching, again and again. And I have gazed at the beaauty of his lotus-face and I have marvelled at the beauty of his life.

He never received what so many of us are proud to call "modern education." Stories and parables and simple words of wisdom, drawn from the "Puranas," and dramas bearing upon Sri Krishna and Sri Chaitanya were dear to him.

Many came to him' asking him to be their guru. He disclaimed the status of a guru. He said he was not a guru, but a servant,-a servant of all human beings. And he said further that Rama and Krishna and Buddhà had breathed their breath in him. He said, too, that the grace of Kali, the Mother Divine, was upon him. The Mother was the Divine Spirit pouring blessings on all races, all religions, all prophets and saints, all teachers and seers of humanity.

Many years ago, I spent a few days in Patna. There I wrote my first little book on Sri Ramakrishna. And they asked me:-- "What think you of Ramakrishna ?" And I Said:- "Ramakrishna, some of you tell me, was not a scholar. But Ramakrishna had wisdom which was more than scholarship." I added:- "Ramakrishna, I love to think of as a flute on the lips of the Lord. and through that flute moved a music for the healing of the nations."

The central note of Ramakrishna's music of the flute was this:- All religion are true and all worship is an offering to God.

Ramakrishna and Keshub Chandra and Vivekanand were among the earliest voices of the wisdom of the *rishis*, in our days. God, they declared, was One but had different names; an all religions had their root in faith, hope and love. Every worship, Ramakrishna taught in his own, simple, child-like way, was a note in the one symphony of life.

Love in all things is God. And Love is Light. Light is Wisdom. Wisdom Is Life,-the Life Divine. And the secret of it, as the Sufis said, again and again, is Beauty.

So , when they asked Ramakrishna, , "What is the way,- the easiest, the simplest and the most effective,-to God?" he answered:-"Bhakti yoga." And when they asked him further, "What is bhakti yoga." he said:- "Union with the Life Divine,-union with the Mother through love."

Of Love Divine, did Ramakrishna become an instrument. Therefore words of wisdom came out of his lips. And men, who listened to him, marvelled.

Not yet hath India, not yet hath the West, realised the spiritual greatness of Ramakrishna's genius. Slowly is the meaning of Ramakrishna's life growing on the thought of the West. The creative genius of this man, who kept far from crowds and the scholar's books,is yet to be realised by India. The realisation will come in the day when the nation understands that it is not yet truly free. True freedom is not political. He is truly free who is released from bondage to the "ego." True freedom is of the Spirit. Ramakrishna lived and moved as a child of the Spirit.

Sri Ramakrishna, again and again, emphasised the great teaching of the "Bhagavad Gita":-"God may be realised by different paths." He said, one day:- "Why do they indulge in quarrels? One says, you cannot attain anything unless you worship Krishna. Yet another says, you cannot gain anything spiritual without the worship of kali the Divine Mother.. Yet there are others who say, you cannot be saved unless you accept the Christian religion." Ramakrishna boldly declared that all this was dogmatism. "It is the dogmatist," he said, "who quarrels in the name of religion, saying:- 'My religion alone is true and the religions of others are false.'"

Ramakrishna's lotus-face was a picture of peace and love. His love went out to all. He realised that God moved in every form. "Yes," said Ramakrishna, "God manifests Himself alike in the sage and in the sinner."

Ramakrishna's teaching was an emanation of his life. Love all, he taught; pray for love, for pure love. And on even those, whom the world discards as sinners, pour love, pure love, nothing but love! There is passage gleaned from the Saint's conversations by a disciple,-a passage, penetrated with such pure beauty that I am tempted to quote it at length:-

To my Divine Mother I prayed only for pure love.

At Her lotus-feet I offered a few flowers and I prayed:-
"Mother! here is virtue and here is vice;
"Take them both from me.
"Grant me only love, pure love for Thee!
"Mother! here is knowledge and here is ignorance;
"Take them both from me.
"Grant me only love, pure love for Thee!
"Mother! here is purity and here is impurity;
"Take them both from me.
"Grant me only love, pure love for Thee!"

In him,-his life and teaching,-the spirit of love was made manifest unto the children of men. In a temple built on a bank of the Hugly river, lived in simplicity and humility and deep reverence for all,-at once for saints and sinners,-he, whom they called Gadadhar Chatterji. This simple man, Gadadhar, drank in more and more of the love of God, until he was intoxicated with love.

This God-intoxicated man was destined to thrill the hearts of men and women in many parts of East and West.

[3]

The story of Sri Ramakrishna is really a story of inner life. His adventures were in the inner realm of the Spirit

A spiritual genius, Ramakrishna was a union of the mystic, prophet, poet, and saint.

The main incidents of his outer life may be briefly told. He was born in February, 1836. He passed on in August, 1886. He was born in a village named Kamarpukar, near Jahanabad, in the Hugli District. He was cremated at the burning ghat, Beranagore, and a beltree stands on the spot where the body of the Blessed One was burnt.

His father, named Khudiram Chatterji, was a brahmin, the head of the only brahmin-family in the village. His mother was named Chandra Devi. Ramakrishna had two brothers and two sisters, himself being the youngest. His proper name was Sambu Chandra. But his father named him Gadadhar,-a name given to Vishnu,-a name which is a symbol of *shakti* or strenght, the literal meaning being "one who holds the club."

They send him to a village-school. He learns to read and write. He hates mathematics. He loves the *kathas* of Ramayana and Mahabharata, the dramas of Krishna, Dhruva and Prahalad , the Vaishnava lyrics and wandering minstrel's songs. This is a period of play and laughter in his life. He moves among the village-folk. He is popular with men and women.

He is hardly seven years of age, when his father dies. Gadadhar has little taste for books. He learns from Nature. He learns from wandering *sadhus*, who tell him stories of heroes and saints. Nature is his teacher. Is not the Earth an interpreter of the Spirit, and Nature richer in inspiration than all schoolmasters? Nature links us with an inner world of health and healing. But our noisy schools so often devitalise us!

At seventeen begins his second period. He is taken from his villag to Calcutta. He assists his brother who is a temple-priest. After his brother's death, Ramakrishna assumes the office of priest in the Dakshineshwar Temple.

Dakshineshwar is a village situated four miles to the north of Calcutta. The Temple was built by Rani Rasmani and is dedicated to kali. She inherited her huge property from her husband and she showed conspicuous ability in managing the property. This wealthy lady was held in high esteem for her energy and courage. One night, English soldiers, drunk with wine, forced their way into her big house to plunder it. It was her singular courage which saved the situation. She opposed the drunken soldiers successfully. They were compelled to quit the place.

The foundation of her life was laid in singular faith in God. Her devotion to Kali was marvellous. She regarded Her as a Living Presence. In invoking Kali, Rani Rasmani felt she was receiving the strength she needed for her daily life.

Her faith in Kali was beautifully blended with her sympathy for the poor. Everyday, she fed a large number of brothers and sisters. She distributed not only food to them but gave them gifts of money and clothes. A colony of fishermen was taxed by the Government. The fishermen came to Rani Rasmani, saying:-"Tax is imposed on us for catching fish in the Ganges. We are too poor to pay any tax. We seek your protection." This great-hearted lady asked the fishermen to carry no anxiety on their hearts. She managed the whole situation so ably and tactfully that the Government was compelled to withdraw the tax on fishing.

Another beautiful trait of her character was her *bhakti.* In her heart was a longing to be a servant of Kali. In the official seal of her estate were engraved the following words:- "Sri Rasmani Devi, longing for the feet of Kali,"

She had a great desire to go to kasi (Banaras) and offer worship there to Vishwanath, the "Lord of the Universe," and Annapurna, the "Divine Mother." Rani Rasmani made preparations to start for kasi in 1849. Her boats, large and small, a hundred in number, were ready. And she actually started and arrived at the village called Dakshineswar. Then, suddenly, she had, in a dream, a vision of Kali. And in the vision, she thought an order came to her from the Goddess to the following effect:- 'Rasmani! Dear Rasmani! Why needst thou go to Kasi? Far-off, indeed, is kasi. Why wilt thou not install my stone-image in a beautiful spot on the bank of this beautiful Bhagirathi, and arrange for My daily worship there, and food-offerings to be given to the poor and all worshippers?"

To Rani Rasmani the vision is a command. She immediately decides not to proceed to Kasi and issues instructions to purchase a very extensive plot at Dakhineswar. She succceeds in buying many acres of land.

Rani Rasmani felt she had in her work the blessings of Kali. And, in 1855, on Thursday, the 31st of may, she rejoiced that her dream was fulfilled. The image of the Divine Mother Kali was installed in the Temple, known as Dakshineshwar Temple. The Temple is surrounded by a spacious garden. Rani Rasmani spent nine lakhs of rupees on the Temple and in addition, she gave a *zemindari* (estate) of two lakhs and a half, for the upkeep of the Temple.

Marvellous are the ways of Providence! Rani Rasmani lived to see the Temple built and the Mother's image istalled. Yet only a day after the Trust Deed of the Temple had been completed, this great and gifted lady, rich in faiht, rich too in love for the poor, passed on to her Great Peace at the feet fo the Divine Mother.

Blessed was she! I love to think of her as a singular devotee of Kali. To Her she dedicated her wealth, her gifts, her life, her all. Her name is impershable, for she was the builder of the Temple where Ramakrishna stayed and wrought the wonder of his life as the Saint of Dakshineswar.

At Dakshineswar, it may be noted, he is for the first tme given the name,-Ramakrishna,-now known the world over. At Dakshineswar, too, he goes through those wonderful experiences which are of profound interest, I believe, to students of the subconscious and the superconscious. This period of twelve years,-from 1855 to 1867,-is a priod of struggle and *sadhanas* in Ramakrishna'life. It is a period of spiritual disciplines and mystical illumination.

The years 1867 to 1885 mark the closing period in Ramakrishna's life. It is a period of his growing influence on the "educated" in Bengal. In this period, the Saint becomes a Teacher of men. What precious truths he teaches through stories and parables and those wonderful saying which I call "Words of wisdom!"

In 1885, he suffers from throat trouble: it develops into cancer. He is removed from Dakshineshwar to Calcutta. He is placed there under the treatment of the famous physician, Dr. Mohendra Lal Sircar. Towards the end of the year, he is removed to a garden-house at Cossipore. There, he quits his body in August, 1886.

Philo, the great Neo-Platonist sage, adored the "Mother of the Creative Word." The Gnostics worshipped the "Divine Sophia" as the "Shining Mother." Of Her, too, sang the poet of Bengal, Bhavani Prasad:- "Thou that revealest Thyself as the All-Pervading Mother, a hundred times do I salute Thee!" And her,the Divine Mother, Ramakrishna saluted on that Sunday, -the last day of *Sravana* is 1886,- as he breathed out the last benediction of his earth-life. Thrice he uttered the Blessed Name of Kali, the Mother. Thrice he saluted Her. Then he sank into Her lap!

The beauty of Ramakrishna's life fascinated an increasing number of men and women. How they travelled to him from cities and villages of Bengal! How they would gaze and gaze at his lotus-face! *Nitya-mukta* was he, said many,-eternally free. But he called himself a servant of humanity. With what reverence in his heart did he not touch the ground which they, who called themselves his disciples, had trodden!

They marvelled at the purity of his life. He had controlled and transformed the sex-impulse. How they wondered at this man whom money could not tempt! When a disciple of his offered him ten thousand rupees, he asked in all humility to be excused. This man, pure in life, peerless in character, was a man of deep humility, And to this man every woman was a mother, a symbol of the one Divine Mother he adored as Kali.

Child-like was he in his tenderness. A saint was he in porfound humility. A *bhakta* of the *bhaktas* was he in the unspeakable sweetness of his words and expression. A divine smile always played upon his lips.

He had his own way of expressing his ideal of life. To him it was not an ideal but a realisation. The supreme truth which he realised in daily life, he one day expressed in two words:-

> *Naham, naham !*
> *Tuhu, Tuhu !*
> (Not I, not I!
> Thou, Thou!)

Yes his "I" was annihilated. His life was merged in the one Divine Thou, the Eternal Thou of the *Atman.* Again and again, they woul come and say to him:- "Master!" Again and again, he answered them in his own gentle, humble way:- "I am nobody's Master: I am everybody's disciple!"

Truly great, unquestionable in their spiritual stature were some of his disciples,-the two greatest of them being, perhaps, Brahmanand and Vivekanand. The influence of both was great on India and travelled beyond India to the Western world. Of Vivekanand, a day after he spoke at the "Parliament of Religions," Chicago, the "New York Herald" wrote:- "Vivekanand is undoubtedly the greatest figure in the Parliament of Religions. After hearing him we feel how foolish it is to send missionaries to this learned nation!" Yet another American journal, "The New York Critique," wrote of Vivekanand the following significant words:- "He is an orator by divine right."

Yes,- Vivekanand's voice was musical, sweet, lyrical.But not many realised that in the music of his voice was the *bhakti,* the love Vivekanand had for his "Master"- Sri Ramakrishna.

Ramakrishna kindled love in the hearts of many, keshub Chandra, the great religious leader of Bengal, was younger than Ramakrishna: how tenderly Ramakrishna loved Keshub! And how intensely did Keshub love Ramakrishna! When Keshub fell seriously ill in Calcutta. Ramakrishna felt so deeply anxious. Ramakrishna always turned to his Divine Mother for help and succour on occasions of anxiety. And Ramakrishna prayed to the Divine Mother for keshub. When a devotee came from Calcutta to meet the Saint in the Dakshineswar Temple, he inquited of Keshub's health, then said to the devotee:- "I made a vow to worship the Mother with green coconut and sugar on Keshub's revovery. And I cried to my Mother:- 'O Mother! make Keshub well again. If Keshub does not live, whom shall I talk to when I go to Calcutta?"

[5]

Years of aspiration, meditation and adoration in silence ripened into a realisation of the Divine Mother. It was a long period of *sadhanas-of* striving, of spiritual disciplines. For twelve years at a stretch, he said one day, he had not a wink of sound sleep: his eyes were denied sleep: they longed to have a vision of the Divine Mother. In that period it was that the yogi, named Totapuri, initiated Gadadhar into *sanyasa* and gave him the new name,-Ramakrishna.

His *sanyasa* was, essentially, inner: he dressed as an ordinary Bengali, and in his daily life of prayer, simplicity and humility, he bore witnes to his absolute devotion to the Mother Divine.

He called Her Kali. "My mother," he said: "Mother of the Universe," he said. And he would talk to Her, as a child to the Mother. I do not know, but it will not, I think, be wrong to say that worship of the Mother is the most ancient religion known to man. When Mohanjo-daro was discovered in Sind, the great archaeologist, Sir John Marshal, announced the discovery that Kali was worshipped in that ancient period of civilisation. Kali-worship and the worship of Siva, he regarded as the most ancient living faith in the world. Kali is a symbol of the two-fold aspect of life:-(1) the Mother's loving care, protection and rapture; and(2) pain and darkness of life.

The thought seized the very centre of Ramakrishna's consciousness that the Spirit Divine that pervaded the whole universe, even as the Spirit, that penetrated through and through the consciousness of man, was the Mother. Again and again, he cried to Her. Again and again, he expressed his intense aspiration to realise each day the presence of the Mother Divine. In pure love and longing would Ramakrishna cry, again and again;- "O Mother! O Mother!"

Swami Vivekanand gives a vivid picture of Ramakrishna's life in its spiritual struggle for a vision of Kali, the MOther, in the following most poignant words:-

"O Mother!" he would cry; "show me the Truth!
"Art Thou there? Art Thou there?
"Dost Thou exist?
"Why then shoul I be left in ignorance?
"Why can I not realise?
"Words and philosophy are vain:
"Vain is all this talk of things.
"Truth!
"It is Truth alone I long to realise.
"Truth I fain would touch.
"Truth is all I wish to feel within me!"

And Truth, Ramakrishna realised mor and more. had its shrine in the heart.

[6]

Enriched, at last, with the wisdom of the heart, Ramakrishna realised (1)the inner unity and (2) the spiritual correspondences of different religions,-their different forms, symbols and sacraments. Henceforth, the illuminated consciousness of Ramakrishna saw the vanity of controversies and quarrels in the name of religion.

Keshub Chandra spoke of "harmony of religions": he realised

that all prophets and saints, all sages and seers, all scriptures and sacraments of different religions were rooted in a vision of the One Truth than which there was no higher Truth open to man-the Truth that is Light, the Truth that is Love. Ramakrishna and Keshub and Vivekanand and Brahmanand were among those blessed few in the modern era to whom the truth came vividly that in all religions was radiant the One Light, as in all prophets and saints worked the One Love divine. Keshub rightly said:- "Our position is not that truths are to be round in all religions but that all the religions of the world are true." Yes,-all religions are revelations of the One Spirit.

This truth came to Ramakrishna not as a theory caught from the words of a book or a scripture, but as a personal realisation of the Life Divine. Ramakrishna longed to know what the essence of Islam was and how it was related to the teaching of the mystics of Islam, *sufis* and *dervishes*. He went and lived with a Muslim *fakir*. Ramakrishna moved in that Muslim mystic's atmosphere. Ramakrishna dressed like a Muslim and lived like a Muslim until the truth of Islam, the truth of Muslim mysticism, flashed upon his soul: he saw and he believed!

So Ramakrishna penetrated to the heart of the Christian Faith. He meditated on Jesus until he saw Jesus in a vision. And for three days together, he only talked of Jesus and sang of him and meditated on him in the heart within. In his vision of Jesus he realised the essence of the Christian Religion.

So, too, the truth of Buddha came to Ramakrishna, not as a theory of boods, not as a dead tradition of a dead past, but as a living, flaming torch, growing and ever growing in a vision of the heart within.

I cannot forget the day when, on visiting Ramakrishna's room, I saw there a statute of Buddha and a picture of Jesus. And I learnt that to Ramakrishna had come,also, a vision of Shyama, Sri Krishna. In that vision he had seen himself as Radha. Since that day, he loved to think of himself, again and again, as Krishna's bride: and he often referred to Shyama as the "beloved."

A rich Bengali at Calcutta,-a disciple of Ramakrishna, -employed a painter to produce a symbolical picture,-one of the most beautiful pictures I have seen, It enshrines the idea of Harmony of

Religions. When this Picture was shown to Keshub, he was filled with joy and he exclaimed:- "Blessed is the man who conceived the idea of this Picture."

In the background of the Picture we see a church, a mosque and a temple. In front of the church stand Keshub and Ramakrishna. Keshub carries the flag of the "New Dispensation,"-the name by which he often expressed his idea of a "religion of harmony."And Ramakrishna, standing by Keshub's side, calls Keshub's attention to the Group of figures in front of the mosque and the temple.

In the middle of the Group we see Christ and Chaitanya dancing together. And round these two,- Jesus and Chaitanya,-stand in the picture(1) a Muslim, (2) a Confucian, (30 a Sikh, (4) a Parsi, (5) an Anglican clergyman, and (6) some Hindus.

It is a Picture truly beautiful for, if the essence of beauty be a perception of the Infinite in form, this Picture is penetrated, through and through, with a perception of the One Divine Spirit pervading at once the outer world and the inner realm,-the one Divine Presence enriching at once the architectures of different religions and the worships and sacraments of diverse faiths. This picture is, in truth, a Teacher, for it is a symbol of the inner harmony of different religions. This picture is a symbol and a revelation! And in this Picture is a beautiful representation of the inner faith, the deepest, profoundest faith of Ramakrishna's heart.

[7]

The essence of this faith is love. God is love. In this faith is the meeting-point of Jesus and Ramakrishna, of Keshub and Brahmanand, of Kabir and Vivekanand, of Tagore and the mystics of Sind.

When they asked Ramakrishna, one day, what was the path which we of the modern age might tread to reach God,-was it *gnana marga* or *karma marga* or *bhakti marga*?- the Saint said:- "The Parth, the *marga* for the age in which we live is *bhakti*"

And Ramakrishna proceeded to point out that *ganana marga* or the path of knowledge was so difficult; it was not easily accessible to all. Who could say he had adequate knowledge of the Infinite, the Endles, the Incomprehensible One? And was not *karma marga*,,- the path of Action,-too, a difficult one? For, to tread the path of *karma* aright, you must renounce all desire for fruits of action. And who could say that he had renounced the desire for all fruits? Man was so weak! In love, Ramakrishna said, in *bhakti*, in devotion, was the secret, which could, with less difficulty, be seized by the average man of the age in which we lived.

Ramakrishna announced another great truth, too. In significant words the saint said:- "Knowledge and love of God are ultimately one. There is no difference between pure knowledge and pure love."For , indeed, when you attain to pure knowledge, which is more than empirical, you move in self-detachment, you renounce desires. And pure love, is it not, also, open only to those who, renouncing appetities and desires, have taken refuge at the feet of the Lord? On the heights, then, knowledge and love meet each other greet each other, and see each other, in the Beauty,-the One Beauty of the Beloved.

True *bhakti*, Ramakrishna said, is Love Divene: he who has it is like a veritable drunkard. It is not exaggeration to say that Ramakrishna's love was like that of a veritable drunkard. Ramakrishna was God-intoxicated. Did I say, in my opening words, that Ramakrishna's name was a music to my ears? Doth it not sing to me thus:-

O Love! all things be from Thee!
O Love! all things be to Thee!
And in all forms of Beauty
In Nature, on Earth and in Heaven
Is Thy radiance, Love!
And to Thee, O Love!
Do all things return,
Even as from Thee do all things emanate
In endless procession!

Never was Ramakrishna tired of repeating this message to all who met him:—"Love God, and in love find the fulfilment of your life!"

And in him shineth the light of love who hath destroyed the ego, who hath cancelled the "I": and becoming a zero, he passes on and enters into "infinity." Cancel the ego: what remains is *Atman*, the Self, the Spirit Divine.

"Who can ever know God?" said Ramakrishna one day. "It is love of God I want."

Loving God, let me learn to love all. Let me love even those who go astray,—the sinners, too, not alone the saints. Let me love the simple and the little ones, love children,—angels on earth.

[8]

The way to reach God in this *yuga*, the *kali-yuga*,—the age of possessions, and power,- Ramakrishna says, again and again, is *bhakti marga*,—the Way of Love. And there are five things asked of everyone who would tread this path,—the path of *bhakti* or love.

(1) Sing God's Name (Nama) and the glories of God (*vibhutis*).

(2) Keep holy company. Be in contact with a *bhakta*, a saint of God, so that you may move, every day and every night, in an atmosphere of purity and aspiration. Else would this world, swayed by sordid things, swallow you.

(3) Every day go into silence and meditate on God, on Kali the Mother, on a saint or a *bhakta*, on the words and deeds of Krishna or Chaitanya, of Jesus or Buddha, of Nanak or Kabir. Retire to a corner, and meditate on this truth, again and again:—"God alone is Real." See, how everything in the world is passing! All things go. Houses, buildings, institutions, kingdoms, empires,—they pass away. Alone the Mother Divine is Real. Meditating thus, in silence and solitude, you will develop what the *rishis* have called *viveka*, discrimination: you will know that all things are *fleeting*, that only the One, the *Atman*, abides: all things pass away.

And all things of the universe, Ramakrishna sums up under two headings,—*kanchan* and *kamini*. *Kanchan* is "gold," is money, is wealth. *Kamini* is woman. *Kanchan* is greed: *kamini* is lust. *Kanchan* is wealth of the world: *kamini* is sex-urge, passion. *Kanchan* and *kamini* both perish. So run not after them! Seek alone what Is Imperishable. Seek the Real, the Abiding, the Eternal.

(4) Do your duty, everyday: but do not forget God! You have

your work to do: you have your family to look after. But see that neither "work" nor "family" absorbs all your time and energies. Your *swadharma* you must do: your duties you must fulfil: but forget not *smaran*. Do your daily work, but keep Hari in your heart!

From a village I brought a cook to serve me, when I was out to beloved Sink. Day after day, he world sit in the kitchen and do his duty. He served me honestly: he cooked for me: but sitting in the kitchen, his face would, again and again, wear, a solemn appearance. "What is the matter?" I asked. And he said to me:—"Sir! here I sit far away from my home. Here I sit and serve: I sit and do my duty: I cook for you: but my thoughts go out, again and again, to my home in the village."

What the servant said is beautifully true. Let me do my duty everyday. But even as in the heart of the cook was a memory of his home in the village in the midst of his daily work, so should I have in my heart, in the midst of all my activities, my daily duties, a remembrance of my true Homeland in the Spirit.

(5) Have a longing in your heart for God! And let that longing reflect itself in tears. People, Ramakrishna says, weep for money, for children, for wife, for honours of the earth. O, asks Ramakrishna, how many weep for God? Weep for the Divine Mother, the Saint says; and She will not leave Her Child. Weep for Her and She will come and greet you and lift you in Her lap.

The deepest longing in Ramakrishna's heart was for communion with the Divine Mother.

Centuries before Ramakrishna trod the soil of India, a great thinker, one of the greatest the world has seen,—Shankara Acharyan,—glimpsed the truth that in *bhakti* was reflected the "true form" of the *Atman*, the Real Self. Shankara said:—"Among the instruments of *mukti*, emancipation, the supreme is *bhakti*, devotion, love."

Ramakrishna loved to think of himself as a pilgrim on the path of love. The prayer of his prayers, his one continuous aspiration, his richest realisation, was God. With every breath of his being he breathed out this one longing:- "Give Thou me Thyself!"

A great Sufi rightly said:-"The first condition of him, who would be a pilgrim on the road of love, is,-make yourself humble as dust and ashes." Ramakrishna, It many be truly said, was humble as dust and ashes, humble as a blade of grass. Ramakrishna's *bhakti* was rich in radiance,-the radiance of humility.

The vision of the "Bhagavad Gita" was verified in the daily life of Ramakrishna;- "Learn to look with an equal eye upon all beings, seeing the One Self in all." And in all did Ramakrishna behold his Divine Mother.

Ramakrishna had learnt to lose himself (1) in the Divine Spirit, and (2) in every form of the Diving Spirit. "When you learn to lose yourself," said a great teacher of the Inner Way, "you will reach the Beloved." And Ramakrishna's joy it was to meet the Beloved everywhere,-in every form, in every manifestation, in sun and rain, in toil and labour, in service and sacrifice, among the lowly and the lost. To Ramakrishna, the Divine Mother Kali was radiant in life, radiant in death. Death, too, was to him a messenger of the Mother, a "friend"of God.

The mystical vision of the One was, in Ramakrishna. blended with the Vaishnava ideal which saw Him in *maya*, too: so was *maya* transformed into *leela*, a play of the Divine Life, an instrument of the Spirit. M*aya* was no longer a bondage of things. *Sansara*, the world. was no more a thing to be shunned. Fetters had fallen. The world became a manifestation of the Divine Mother.

[9]

Most marvellous experiences came to Ramakrishna in the unfolding of his interior life. Suddenly, it dawned upon him that he was Radha, the beloved of Krishna. And for some days, Ramakrishna wore Radha's dress: in a trance he saw Krishna,- the Beloved. Ramakrishna realised he was not in bondage to matter, to things or phenomena: he was free, a *mukta*, a *nitya-mukta*. And he realised the richness of his unity with the poor, the outcast, the fallen, the sinner. He was born in a brahmin family: henceforth, he felt he was one with the outcast. the *chandala*. Ramakrishna began to do the scavenger's work: and he began to take food given to beggars and *chandals*. He cleansed the temple like an outcast during the night: and he ate the fragments of food left by beggars at the temple.

The supreme vision of the One-in-all filled his heart: he would bow down before prostitutes and ask them to bless him. Ramakrishna rejoiced in being a worshipper of the poor and the lowly, The outcasts were not strangers to him. The broken ones became his brothers.

They asked me, what I thought was the "religion of Ramakrishna." Was it Vedanta? Was it Saivism? Was it the Hindu Faith? Was it the Faith of the Muslim *fakir* or the Christian saint? Was it the Faith of the Buddhist *arhat*, the Faith of the Bodhisatva who would not enter into *nirvana* until all creatures had been saved?In answer to the question, I said:- "Ramakrishna's religion was the Religion of Love.'And they, indeed, who love, have no religion but the Divine Mother! The supreme message of Ramakrishna to modern India and the modern world is this message of harmony, unity, love.

Ramakrishna taught the truth that if we would, indeed, see God, and serve God, we must look into the heart within. Therefore, (1)must the heart be lowly; and (2) the heart must be kindled with the fire of love. In East and West, everywhere, there is piteous need, today, not of intellectuals, not of industrialists, not of technological institutes, not of an external, superficial "civilisation" of money and the machine,-the most urgent need, today, is of burning hearts,-hearts that are humble and lowly and radiant with love. Burning hearts, not men of power and posessions, will lay the foundation of a new peace movement and be, in a quiet, humble way, the builders of a new brotherly civilisation.

The great Persian mystic, Rumi, in a beautiful poem, tells us of how, one day Moss, the Prophet, sees a shepherd on the way, crying:- "O Lord! where art Thou? I long to serve Thee and comb Thy hair and wash Thy clothes and kill Thy lice and bring milk to Thee and kiss Thy little hand and rub Thy little feet and sweep Thy little room at night before Thou dost retire."

Moses, the Prophet, hearing these words is greatly annoyed and quidkly he speaks rough words to the shepherd:-"O foolishman! To whom are you speaking these foolish words? What blasphemy are you uttering? Better that you were stricken dumb than that you should speak thus to God the Most High. Thy words are a crime,

O shepherd! Put cotton into your mouth and speak no longer a word of irreverence to thy Lord who, in a moment, can consume thee to ashes and dust."

And the shepherd, we are told, rends his garment in agony and heaves a sigh and goes quickly forth into the wilderness.

Then unto Moses comes a revelation at night. To Moses speaks the Lord:-"Moses! thou wert sent into the world to unite, not to sever. But you have parted form Me My servant, My devotee. Dear to Me is that shepherd. Forget not, Moses! that every mode of worship is Mine. The modes are many: religions are many: yet all are Mine. Each one has his own path, his own way, his own form, his own idiom. Moses! I look not at tongue and words: I look at the spirit and the inward feeling."

And Moses goes out to meet the shepherd and says to him:-"I repent! And I ask thee to forgive me!"

I love to think of Ramakrishna, as I do of the *rishis*, as sent to unite, not to sever. Verily, Ramakrishna was of the race of the *rishis*, who made India truly vital in the long ago.

Thinking of Ramakrishna, I say to myself:- "Were not Ramakrishna and Goethe's Faust poles apart?"Ramakrishna discarded "civilisation." *kanchan* and *kamini*, and turned to self-control and *bhakti* or love for the wisdom which is in the heart. Faust wandered from one realm of human knowledge to another in his quest for Truth, and at the end exclaimed.-"Here am I , at last, a very fool, with useless learning crust, no wiser than at first!" Faust was filled with despair, then opened an ancient book and saw the seal of Solomon, and understood that the Earth was interpenetrated with Heaven, and Faust exclaimed:- "I feel the dawn of youth again."

God fills the universe,-*Ishavasyam sarvam idam*! In this truth is the Light revealed to Ramakrishna . He saw the Light,-the One Light of God,-in all religions and races, in all scriptures and symbols, in all men,- sinners and saints.

Ramakrishna's teaching may well be summed up thus: -(1) In all is radiant the One Light. (2) This Light shines in the Heart and in the little ones,-in children and in *satpurukhas*: the same Light shines in Nature, in *samsara* and *maya*. (3) You, too, may see the

Light, if you will but learn to withdraw the "veils,"-the many "veils" of LIght. This withdrawal is detachment. (4) Truth shines for him who has learnt to walk the way of "detachment" or desirelessness,-out of which are the three great qualities of integrity, purity and compassion or love.

Ramakrishna saw the One Light in all religions. Therefore, he bowed in reverence to all prophets and saints. Therefore were dear to him all religions: none was an exclusive revelation of Truth: nonw was the only Path to God; each was but a few Rays of the Divine Light.

Therefore, let all religions live in harmony, one with the other, and let all nations live in peace, one with the other. Each is a flower in the Garden of God: each is a note in the One Music, the One Symphony of the Spirit.

Words Of Wisdom

[*''Sayings'' of Sri Ramakrishna*]

And now I see His beauty
Moves in every human form:
He reveals Himself
Alike in the sinner and the sage.

*

Wilt thou enter into divine illumination?
Then must thou be simple as a child!

*

Like unto a miser
Who longeth still for gold,
Let thy heart long and long for the Lord!

*

The strength of the seeker is in his tears:
Weep and win the Lord!

*

As a lamp cannot burn without oil,
So a man cannot live without God!
I see the whole world full of the Lord from end to end!

*

I know not logic-chopping:
I only know I am a child of the Mother Divine!

*

As the sun in a mirror clear
So in the pure ones shines the Lord.

*

Family-life, too, is blessed. It is as a fort. Easier it is to fight the enemy from within than outside the fort.